WORLD-CLASS ENDORSEMENTS

"*The Champion's Mind* reveals the mental skills and strategies Olympic champions use to perform their best when it matters most. Dr. Afremow's matchless book is a must for athletes and coaches."

—SHANNON MILLER, Olympic gold medalist in gymnastics
and president of Shannon Miller Lifestyle

"I read this book with my eyes wide open, and the content continued to keep them open at all times. Jim's advice and tips are very simple and easy to understand. Read only one chapter at a time and apply it to your approach to tennis, sports, and life."

—NICK BOLLETTIERI, founder and president
of Nick Bollettieri IMG Tennis Academy

"*The Champion's Mind* is a mental training book that will help you reach your potential in sports. I highly recommend this book to all athletes and coaches."

—JACKIE SLATER, NFL Hall of Famer

"How sweet it is to breathe that rarefied air of a high-performance athlete! How refreshing it is, as well, to recognize so many of the techniques in Dr. Afremow's book that get you to that privileged place. *The Champion's Mind* is a simple, straightforward elixir for the high achiever in all of us."

—MORTEN ANDERSEN, NFL's all-time leading scorer and a member
of the NFL's All-Decade Teams for the 1980s and 1990s

"*The Champion's Mind* is loaded with great lessons, advice, and perspectives on how to be successful. It is definitely not a requirement to be an athlete or a coach in order to benefit from this book. The skills and strategies that Jim provides here are essential in carving a path to success, no matter what field you are in or what your goals are. I can honestly say that I have lived by many of the strategies offered in this book, and I can also say I wish I had lived by more of them. But it's never too late to be as good as you can be!"

—DAN JANSEN, Olympic gold medalist in speed skating
and former world record holder

"What tends to differentiate the all-stars from the rest of the pack resides between the ears. Jim Afremow does a great job exploring this subject in *The Champion's Mind*. This is a great book for coaches and athletes of all ages who are looking to improve performance at any level, in any sport."

—SHAWN GREEN, two-time MLB All-Star

"Dr. Afremow nails all the basics and gives readers an excellent window into how a champion's mind works before and during 'the process.'"

—RANDY CROSS, three-time Super Bowl Champion

"The mind is a powerful thing. As a baseball player, the more confidence I have and the more mentally prepared I am, the better I perform when it matters the most. *The Champion's Mind* will help guide you to reach your potential both on and off the field!"

—TRAVIS BUCK, MLB outfielder, San Diego Padres

"Athletes who want to learn the secrets of the mental game should read *The Champion's Mind.*"

—CARLI LLOYD, two-time Olympic gold medalist and 2008 U.S. Soccer Female Athlete of the Year

"One can always learn from others. *The Champion's Mind* holds a wealth of insight as to how you can become a winner in your everyday life."

—PHIL MAHRE, Olympic gold medalist in alpine skiing

"It's amazing to see how Dr. Afremow points out what athletes go through every day. He describes a lot of situations that I have experienced as well. In this book, you can find a lot of simple but very useful tips and principles that might help you improve your performance."

—BRITTA HEIDEMANN, three-time Olympian in épée fencing and gold medalist at the 2008 Beijing Olympics

"*The Champion's Mind* is very informative and full of great principles and guidelines for any athlete who is searching for excellence in their performance."

—MIKE CANDREA, Olympic gold medal coach of the U.S. softball team and eight-time national champion coach of the University of Arizona women's softball team

"Athletes can unlock a new level of performance by learning the power of training their mind as they train their body. From preparation to rehabilitation to competition, *The Champion's Mind* gives the mental guidance necessary to allow an athlete to reach their full athletic potential. Dr. Afremow's playbook for increasing mental strength gives clear direction to make the reader a better athlete, a better teammate, and a better person."

—CURT TOMASEVICZ, Olympic gold medalist in four-man bobsled

"We all have an athlete in us; we were all born to run, jump, swim, and compete in some way or another. The gold medal at an Olympic Games has been declared as the highest honor to reward discipline, commitment, power, strength, finesse, passion, precision, patience, speed, and skill, just to name a few. You too can go for gold in all areas of your life by following Jim's strategies. Decide what you want and go after it with all you have to give, every single day. Daily acts of excellence are the secret. Choose your success today."

—NATALIE COOK, five-time Olympian in beach volleyball
and gold medalist at the 2000 Sydney Olympics

"Do you want to learn how the best in the world got there? In *The Champion's Mind,* Jim distills a myriad of golden Olympic stories into clear tools we all can use. I am positive that you will read insights in this book that will help you rise to the top of your discipline. If you read this book, you will be inspired. Thank you, Jim, for writing this book!"

—ADAM KREEK, two-time Olympian in men's eight rowing
and gold medalist at the 2008 Beijing Olympics

"When I read *The Champion's Mind,* it quite frankly reminded me of many instances, mannerisms, and thoughts leading to my Olympic championship, and it has given me many other wisdoms to pass on to the athletes I now coach. Choose your path, follow your path; any path worth choosing will have its ups and downs, but *The Champion's Mind* will help you with ideas to keep moving forward on that path. The focus you gain will help you reach the top of whatever you seek."

—NICK HYSONG, Olympic gold medalist in the pole vault

"Dr. Afremow hits a grand slam with *The Champion's Mind.* Every athlete should keep a copy of this book in their locker or gym bag."

—LEAH O'BRIEN-AMICO, three-time Olympic gold medalist
for the U.S. softball team

"Dr. Afremow's training and tips have been an important part of the preparation and success of our athletes when they take the Wonderlic test at the NFL combine. In *The Champion's Mind,* Dr. Afremow provides simple yet powerfully effective strategies to help athletes and coaches reach their full potential."

—MARK VERSTEGEN, founder and president
of Athletes' Performance and Core Performance

THE
CHAMPION'S
MIND

THE
CHAMPION'S
MIND

HOW GREAT ATHLETES
THINK, TRAIN,
AND
THRIVE

JIM AFREMOW, PhD

FOREWORD BY JIM CRAIG, GOALIE FOR
THE 1980 U.S. "MIRACLE ON ICE" HOCKEY TEAM

RODALE

© 2013 by Jim Afremow

Trade hardcover first published by Rodale Inc. in January 2014.

Rodale books may be purchased for business or promotional use
or for special sales. For information, please write to:
Special Markets Department, Rodale, Inc.,
733 Third Avenue, New York, NY 10017

Printed in the United States of America
Rodale Inc. makes every effort to use acid-free ♾, recycled paper ♻.

Book design by Christopher Rhoads

Library of Congress Cataloging-in-Publication Data
is on file with the publisher.
978-1-62336-148-8 hardcover
978-1-62336-562-2 paperback

Distributed to the trade by Macmillan

18   20   19   paperback

We inspire and enable people to improve their lives and the world around them.
rodalebooks.com

To my wife, Anne,
and our daughter, Maria Paz

You were born to be a player.
You were meant to be here.
This moment is yours.

—HERB BROOKS,
coach of the 1980 U.S. Olympic "Miracle on Ice" team

CONTENTS

FOREWORD

BY JIM CRAIG

Most people remember me as the goalie from the 1980 Olympic "Miracle on Ice" hockey team. Since then, I have gone on to have a successful sales career of more than 30 years and have become a sought-after motivational speaker and sales trainer. I travel the country delivering my messages on winning teamwork and how to achieve success in business.

Jim got in touch with me after reading my book, *Gold Medal Strategies: Business Lessons from America's Miracle Team*. It combines my years of sales experience and training with the discipline skills I used during the Olympics and my NHL career. As I am a gold medalist and experienced sales trainer, Jim wanted my thoughts on his book.

I was enthusiastic about taking a look at Jim's book because I have long recognized the importance that the mind plays in getting to the top of the podium. *The Champion's Mind* is thoughtful, accessible, and engaging. The chapters are clear and straightforward, and they easily allow the athlete to put Jim's suggestions into action right away.

Jim provides expert advice and proven mental techniques for building a step-by-step improvement plan to accomplish your goals. He does a great job of teaching. He tells you how you too can become a champion in all aspects of your game and perform optimally at the most important time. His suggestions are clear and very readable and easy to remember.

My wife and I have a teenage son and daughter, and they both play sports. To help them increase their enjoyment of athletics and improve their performance, I often share with them my favorite quotes and tips that I have collected on sports and living life. I keep a jar at home filled with these quotes and tips written on pieces of paper and encourage my kids to pull out and practice a lesson every day.

Whether you are an athlete, a parent, or a coach, think of this book you now hold in your hands as your own personal peak-performance jar because *The Champion's Mind* is filled to the brim with golden lessons you will draw on again and again to maximize your athletic potential. So keep this book handy—in your gym bag or locker—and reach for it any time you need inspiration or you want a great opportunity to practice your mental skills. Building your mental game can be as simple as reading a few pages of *The Champion's Mind* before practice or when you are riding on the team bus thinking about the next performance.

Start transforming your game from good to gold medal today. You'll be glad you did.

INTRODUCTION:
IF YOU CAN SPOT GREATNESS,
YOU'VE GOT GREATNESS

Don't envy the champion—be the champion.

The challenging plan presented in this book details how you can reach your pinnacle of athletic excellence and become a champion in your sport or fitness activity, whether you are a high school, college, recreational, professional, or an Olympic athlete. It means you will be vitally engaged in all areas of your game and life by doing your best at what you value most. You will get the job done and rise to the occasion in your championship moments.

Think about the active people in your life, those you respect and hold in high regard. What specific character traits do you value most in these friends, teammates, and coaches? Who in your life has a high IQ in mental toughness?

Also consider your personal athletic heroes, now and throughout history—the Olympians, professional athletes, adventurers, and extreme sports participants. Who specifically do you respect the most and what is their strongest attribute that you admire the most—their confidence, concentration, composure, commitment, or some other attribute?

The same positive mental qualities you admire in others are also within you and waiting to be fully expressed. Perhaps you watched when Tony Womack hit an RBI double off of Yankees' pitcher Mariano Rivera in the bottom of the ninth inning of Game 7 of the 2001 World Series and you thought, "I would love to be that clutch." Maybe you've watched Tiger Woods at the Masters striding down the fairways with total poise as the Sunday leader and you raved, "I wish I could have that level of comfort and confidence on the links."

If you can spot greatness in someone else, then you already have some of that greatness within you, because only a person with similar traits can recognize those traits in others. Think, "If I can spot it, I've got it!"

Admiration and envy are our common psychological responses when watching extremely successful people perform at extremely difficult times. However, our responses can also make others seem superior, but they're not. Still, most of us too quickly dismiss the idea that we could be like or even surpass the heroes we admire and respect the most.

Instead, we must realize that all people are more alike than different, so we're all capable of the mental greatness we see and appreciate in others. Rather than merely trying to mimic these qualities, why not seek *your* fullest expression of *your* positive aspects and attributes and become like the champions you admire?

Living this attitude and striving for your own personal best are how you *champion yourself*, which is the kind of excellence outlined in this book. The main objective for you is to maximize your athletic potential by developing a champion's mind-set. To paraphrase one of Yogi Berra's insightful gems: Sports are 90 percent mental, and the other half is physical. If you want to play like the best athletes, then you have to think like them. Achieving this goal requires a program of psychological preparation and interconnected mental skills, mental strategies, and golden wisdom.

The chapters in this book are organized in short, succinct sections for today's busy athletes, coaches, and parents. Each chapter offers important steps for winning the mental game, so you will start thinking and acting the right way, right away. These tips are no-nonsense, to-the-point techniques for all ages and all goals. These winning attitudes and behaviors are also important life skills for corporate and academic environments, as well as for daily activities.

Mental game pointers and lessons from world-class athletes are provided. You will also hear directly from several gold medalists whose winning mentality helped them triumph in the Olympic crucible. The book presents nine "golden reflections" through personal and inspirational stories from U.S. and international Olympic champions who won in summer or winter sports. Each athlete discusses his or her frame of mind when training and competing for Olympic gold. You will learn how to think, feel, and act like a champion as preparation for accomplishing your highest athletic and fitness goals.

The suggestions in this book are based on classic studies and the latest research findings in performance psychology, as well as on my own extensive professional experiences in sports psychology, where I learned what really works. Read one chapter each day—or one suggestion each reading—to fully absorb the contents. Then you'll be on your way to reaching your truest and fullest potential. You'll be your own champion.

Let the games begin!

CHAPTER ONE

BE YOUR OWN CHAMPION

**The attitude with which we approach the situation
can determine our success or failure.**

—PEYTON MANNING

What separates the top few from the many in a sport? *Mentality.* The importance of the mental side of athletics was once brilliantly summed up by basketball legend Kareem Abdul-Jabbar: "Your mind is what makes everything else work." Tennis great Novak Djokovic further explains: "[Among the] top 100 players, physically there is not much difference. . . . It's a mental ability to handle the pressure, to play well at the right moments."

So your mental game matters the most. Physical ability alone rarely translates into a superior on-field performance. Even naturally gifted athletes who want to perform to their total potential need outstanding physical and mental strengths, because their secret to great performances is not their innate athleticism or technical skills—it's their minds.

Top athletes are often distinguished, especially in the media, by their unique natural gifts. For example, Michael Phelps, the greatest Olympic swimmer, has the wingspan of an albatross, tennis star Roger Federer has the timing of an exquisite Swiss watch, and

Olympic sprinter and world-record holder Usain Bolt is built out of lightning-rod-like twitch fibers.

Behind the scenes, their mind-set and work ethic have enhanced their natural abilities. If you aspire to be a champion, don't be awed by the glitter of their excellence; instead, know that they also put in many thousands of hours in the pool, on the court, and at the track to build up their bodies and shape their minds.

Distance runner Paavo Nurmi, dubbed the "Flying Finn" and the winner of nine Olympic gold medals (including five at the 1924 Paris Olympics), declared, "Mind is everything. Muscle—just pieces of rubber. All that I am, I am because of my mind." You, too, can develop the mental focus and discipline needed to perform in your sport with a champion's mind. The mental abilities of confidence, concentration, and composure are crucial for being a champion in everything you undertake, be it work or sports or both.

In contrast to your physical abilities, your mental abilities may flutter moment to moment, because your mind is susceptible to performance pressures and situational demands. This being true, you cannot trust your athletic performance to chance. Just as you can build physical strength through training, you can also build mental strength through training. Mental dexterity must be practiced and developed in a planned and purposeful manner so that you can elevate yourself to a champion performance level in all endeavors.

Champion yourself. We all experience similar struggles and deal with demanding challenges in our pursuit of excellence, regardless of the sport or fitness activity. To be a champion, your true best self becomes key to personal and athletic greatness. You know, as we all do, that only those performers who think gold and never settle for silver will continue to strive for and reach their highest, or gold, level. A champion *makes* greatness happen, despite what may seem like impossible odds.

Of course most of us are not Olympians or professional athletes.

But all of us can acquire a champion's mind-set. Any athlete can learn to think like a champion. Every one of us can be peak performers in the game of life by achieving our own personal best. We can strive to be the best version of ourselves. It is possible for us to stay "professional" whenever adversity strikes. It is possible to ingrain mental fortitude that drives us forward. And it is possible to take a championship approach.

Part of this process requires us to maintain our eagerness to learn and grow, and to take well-trained, disciplined action to make solid change in our lives.

Sadly, only a small number of people qualify for the Olympics or become professional athletes; so few people ever champion themselves and win with the best version of themselves. This truth is hard to acknowledge, but if you do and if you want your personal championship in life badly enough, then the ball is in your hands. Now the question becomes, will you run with the ball or will you drop it?

Understand that the difference between a pedestrian performance and a peak performance begins and ends with your state of mind. Importantly, all of us *can* learn to think like a champion, but *will* we? Adopting a winning mind-set will help you perform at the top of your game and enable you to succeed when you want to succeed the most. You have hidden inner potential to tap into in order to unleash your inner champion.

A winning mind-set unlocks your athletic aptitude in competition. Champions develop and maintain a complete body *and* mind approach to their performance—the perfect blend of mentality, athleticism, and technique. They enthusiastically make the best of every situation, consistently put in the hard work, and take the extra time needed to realize their aspirations.

Compile a personal scouting report. As an athlete, compile your own scouting report about yourself by taking a hard, unblinking look at all aspects of your performance. To begin, think about the mentality, athleticism, technique, and strategy that go into your performance. How would you rate yourself in these four areas? How would others rate you? Be sure to stay upbeat, because a negative attitude, poor effort, or an unwillingness to improve your conditioning, technique, and strategy will leave you in the bleachers instead of on the medal podium.

Table 1 shows that champions strive endlessly to reach their best level by improving their mind-set, fitness, mechanics, and game strategy. Even if you are a great natural athlete, you still have to tap into that talent. Even if you are on a winning team, you will have to continue to push onward and believe that you can improve. "No coach or team thinks in terms of happy or comfort—those are not words that exist. You keep competing, executing, and trying to improve. It doesn't matter if you have the best record or the worst record," says Gregg Popovich, head coach of the NBA's San Antonio Spurs.

Which level are you committed to reaching—bronze, silver, or

TABLE 1: Excellence always requires an Olympian effort.

	PSYCHOLOGICAL (MIND-SET)	PHYSICAL (FITNESS/ STRENGTH)	TECHNICAL (PROPER MECHANICS)	TACTICAL (GAME STRATEGY)
BRONZE	Good	Good	Good	Good
SILVER	Better	Better	Better	Better
GOLD	Best	Best	Best	Best

gold? No matter your current performance level, never rule out your capacity to become a champion in your game and in your life. You can do better. You can achieve your true potential. It is possible to make a major impact on your own life by shifting your beliefs and expectations about what you can achieve. Attitude is a decision, and it is also a learned behavior, requiring discipline and energy to sustain.

To perform at a champion's level, think of gold as your official color of excellence. Look at your personal and athletic efforts through gold-tinted lenses. Think about personal gold as both a reward and a color of action or prompt to bring out your best qualities and performance. Olympic wrestling champion Jordan Burroughs says, "All I see is gold." It is his mantra. Like Burroughs, look on the more positive side of events and always shoot for the most favorable outcome.

Whether you are a student-athlete, a weekend warrior, a professional athlete, or a serious contender for the Olympics, going gold today will allow you to work to achieve superior performance and gain a genuine competitive advantage. Striving for the highest level will give you the best shot for personal greatness. We all deserve to shine and be successful, but we can achieve this only through intelligently applied hard work.

Recognize that there will never be a better time and place than right now and right here to become a champion in your own game and life. To paraphrase Bob Dylan: You are either busy being born or busy dying. Let's get busy achieving your athletic goals. Put on your own gold medal performance, whether you are going to the gym, running trails, or stepping on the gridiron in a championship game. Why settle for anything less? Consider:

- Don't have the time? You are worth the time!
- Don't have the energy? You will gain energy!
- Doubt yourself? Start doubting your doubt!

THE CHAMPION QUESTION

Champions aren't made in the gyms.
Champions are made from something they have
deep inside them—a desire, a dream, a vision.

—MUHAMMAD ALI

What will your life look like when you have become your own champion? This is the key champion question. Take some time right now to imagine that a major performance breakthrough in your game and life has just occurred and that you have become a champion all day, every day. In your mind's eye, work your way through a regular weekday, a practice or training session, and a future competition. Draw together as much detail as possible about what it will look like to be at a gold level, to be the best version of yourself consistently. What specific actions or behaviors do you see yourself doing better or differently?

Now that you have reshaped and redefined your game, what do you think others will perceive? What do you want them to observe? What would really surprise your teammates, coaches, or competitors? If you could step outside yourself and examine your new performance, what would you recognize in your new attitude and behaviors?

Identify precisely what you do that hurts your own cause the most. Eliminate that action or viewpoint immediately. To perform at a champion's level, you must break any bad habits, such as a tendency to arrive late to practice or just going through the motions when you get there. We are all champions until we lose to ourselves.

Make your new gold story compelling, one that is active and personal. You need to see it to achieve it. Each time you do this exercise, your vision of how you perform as a champion will become clearer and stronger. Your new mental picture will get the performance ball rolling in the right direction.

To go a step further, it is good to contrast the personal pride and peace of mind that results from having a champion approach to life with the future pain and regret of knowing in your heart that you settled for less than your best. Will you continue to sacrifice what you most want to achieve in your game for what is comfortable in the moment? Or will you keep putting your best foot forward, especially when you feel like doing it the least?

My favorite description of what excellence in the sports world looks like comes from Anson Dorrance, the legendary University of North Carolina women's soccer coach. He was driving to work early one morning, and as he passed a deserted field, he noticed one of his players off in the distance doing extra training by herself. He kept driving, but he later left a note in her locker: "The vision of a champion is someone who is bent over, drenched in sweat, at the point of exhaustion when no one else is watching." The young woman, Mia Hamm, would go on to become one of the greatest players in the history of the sport.

Having a big dream—and a clear vision of what you will look like while pursuing competitive excellence—always inspires greatness. What is your dream goal? What does excellence in your game look like when you are fully dialed in and passionately pursuing your dream—becoming the best you can be in your sport? Make the description vivid and powerful enough to give you that burst of adrenaline when you need it, a burst that can come only from connecting completely with your heart's true desire.

Dame Kelly Holmes, a British track star, held on tight to her athletic dreams when she was faced with personal hardships and physical hassles. Specifically, Holmes had to prevail over both

depression and physical injury to shine on sport's biggest stage—
striking gold in both the 800-meter and the 1500-meter races at the
2004 Athens Olympics. In her book *Just Go For It! 6 Simple Steps to
Achieve Success,* this double gold medalist explains the importance of
always thinking in terms of possibilities: "We would accomplish
many more things if we did not think of them as impossible. A
dream is not impossible, so go get yours!"

ACT LIKE YOU'RE A CHAMPION

Be great in act, as you have been in thought.

—WILLIAM SHAKESPEARE

There is no golden road to excellence; excellence is the golden
road. Until you start down this road, you'll never have a chance of
getting there. As such, act as if you are a total champion for set
amounts of time each day by exceeding normal expectations. This
time is where the rubber meets the road. You are confident,
focused, energized, and in charge.

How does it feel different when performing at peak levels versus
just doing business as usual? Are you arriving early to practice or
running late? Are you making weekly plans for training or just
winging it because you're too tired or too busy? Are you giving the
extra effort needed for excellence?

A nonmedalist says, "One day I will," whereas a gold medalist
does it and says, "Today I did." Sergey Bubka of Ukraine, a record-
setting pole-vaulter and gold medalist at the 1988 Seoul Olympics,
always advocated others to "Do it. Then say it." Actions really do

speak louder than words, so take a moment right now to ask your-self, "Am I walking (or running) the talk with how I'm preparing myself for competition?"

Some days you will not feel motivated or your nerves will have gotten the best of you. You will feel as though you have only your B- or C-game ready. This moment will be your moment of truth. Imagine, for example, that you are experiencing prepractice dread. Resolve to spend the first 30 minutes attacking your workout with enthusiasm, as if you really do love it. Most of the time you will continue in the same manner because you will be rolling along and achieving and feeling better than you did.

The best and quickest solution for overcoming your inner resis-tance, challenging old patterns, and changing bad habits is to fake it until you either find your A-game and recover your form or fin-ish it, and the game has ended. Slow it down and break it down. Panic is not an option for a champion.

Doing the one thing you don't want to do (going to the gym/ sticking to your nutrition plan) rather than giving in to your fears/ anxiety by clinging to the familiar (putting the workout off until tomorrow/eating the whole pizza) is your decision at the fork in the road that will determine whether you accomplish your sports goals. Realize that this choice is your choice—you can either act like a champion or take the path of least resistance and not feel chal-lenged.

Push right through your impasse. Stand tall and walk strong. Keep your head in the game. Maximize your mental resources. Eventually you will develop positive new ways of being and per-forming that will become automatic in their own right. This strat-egy is a game changer that will rewire you with peak behaviors and emotions. Acting like a champion really works if you work at it. So go work at it now.

BRING IT EVERY DAY

It's not every four years. It's every day.

—MOTTO OF THE UNITED STATES OLYMPIC COMMITTEE

Chip Kelly, head football coach of the NFL's Philadelphia Eagles, acquired a compelling team motto when he coached the University of Oregon Ducks to unprecedented success: "Win the day." This means you should take advantage of the opportunity that each day brings to be the best athlete you can be. "If you're not getting better, you're getting worse" is a winning philosophy that must be embraced to reach personal excellence and competitive greatness. Peak performance is the daily strike zone we are aiming for.

Excellence can be achieved only *today*—not yesterday or tomorrow, because they do not exist in the present moment. Today is the only day you have to flex your talents and maximize your enjoyment. Your challenge is to win in all aspects of life. To reach that goal, you need to set yourself up for success by winning one day at a time. Procrastination is no match for a champion.

Setting daily goals and striving to achieve them is how you reach the status of a champion. How are you getting better *today*? What will you achieve *today*? Nonmedalists have a yesterday attitude by dwelling on things that didn't go well in a previous performance or a tomorrow attitude by procrastinating and not getting things done *now*.

Mark Spitz swam in two Olympic Games (1968, 1972), where he won a dazzling nine gold medals plus a silver and a bronze. He is the first athlete to win seven gold medals in a single Olympics, a staggering feat only exceeded 36 years later by Michael Phelps, who won eight gold medals at the 2008 Olympics. Spitz understood the importance of focusing on daily acts of excellence. He stated,

"I'm trying to do the best I can. I'm not concerned with tomorrow, but with what goes on today."

Be like Chip Kelly and Mark Spitz by incorporating a "win the day" approach, whether that means getting in extra practice, protecting your rest and recovery time, or crushing it on the field. This is your sporting experience—be vitally engaged and take responsibility for getting the most from it. Today's a brand-new opportunity to go for gold. Don't get derailed. Stay focused.

What do you need to do today to put yourself in a more favorable, positive athletic position? As a champion, you should never settle for less than you can be, but you must also realize that you do not need to be disciplined every second of the day. You only need to be disciplined for those few key moments during the day when you need to avoid temptation and/or start a positive action. To perform at a champion's level, recognize when it is critical to maintain discipline and when it is time to relax—that is, to clear your mind and enjoy your downtime. What are your main temptations to avoid? What are your most positive actions to start?

Recognize that there are some moments during competition that require iron self-discipline, but there are other moments where it is best to take a breather. For example, a golfer must be disciplined when it is time to follow his preshot routine (mind on golf); however, during the time between shots, he can open his focus and relax while he walks down the fairway (mind off golf).

Use the phrase "Think gold and never settle for silver" as your mantra for self-discipline during the moments when discipline is absolutely required. For example, consider shouting, "Think gold!" (or "Personal best!") to yourself—or imagine hearing these words booming from a loudspeaker—whenever you have an important choice to make, such as in the morning when you are deciding whether to hit the snooze button and keep sleeping on a cold, rainy day or to get out of bed and train for your sport.

YOUR DAILY GUT CHECK QUESTIONS

When I go to sleep at night I'm a better martial artist
than when I woke up in the morning.

—GEORGES ST-PIERRE,
UFC WELTERWEIGHT CHAMPION

At sunrise, ask yourself,

"How will I be a champion today?"

(INTENTIONS)

At sunset, ask yourself,

"How was I a champion today?"

(ACCOUNTABILITY)

THE CHAMPION'S WILL-DO-NOW LIST

Organize your life around your dreams—
and watch them come true.

—ANONYMOUS

To perform at a champion's level, you must have a winning off-field game plan that includes specific strategies—for instance, well-placed environmental cues that you can use to achieve excellence and to remind yourself that you are working to win. Tape a note that says, "Think gold and never settle for silver" somewhere noticeable and make it the desktop background on your computer to motivate you to start and continue your day with a winning mind-set.

Think gold and never settle for silver.

Schedule automatic, electronic "think gold" or "personal best" reminders throughout the day; for example, set the reminder function on your cell phone to chime at certain times and display "Champion." If at specific times during the day you feel fatigued or vulnerable to distractions—time-waster stuff on the Internet, junk food, or alcohol—then schedule your "think gold" electronic reminder for these times.

Time management is priority management. Prioritizing your time, whether you are a student-athlete, professional athlete, or weekend warrior, should be a vital part of your daily and weekly game plans. For example, outline your agenda—your pursuit of a championship—each day. Make good choices regarding how you invest your time, energy, and resources. *Champions are on time and on mind for every practice every day.* This allows them to be consistently successful.

Always remember the key word *fun,* and include some fun in your daily activities, as a little fun goes a long way in a satisfying and successful life. Whatever activities or hobbies you enjoy, enjoy them. In return, you'll get renewed energy from these mental time-outs and achieve excellence. Champions know that no one is going to live their life, do their training, or compete for them. Champions are champions because they take charge of their lives and do what they deem best for themselves.

Schedule the right number of daily challenges. An unrealistic plan is a self-defeating plan. Undoable plans are disheartening, so schedule a reasonable number of tasks. At sunset, savor what you've done, albeit done so far.

Daily agendas and to-do lists are excellent tools to help you achieve maximum efficiency and productivity. But try not to have many fillers or unimportant items on your list. To perform at a champion's level, your to-do list has to be a *will-do-now* list.

You are stronger than the initial discomfort experienced in staying disciplined while working hard or changing habits. To achieve positive outcomes, imagine the good feeling of striking off each item on your list. Life is a series of choices, and time is treasure. That being true, own your game by making good choices and using time wisely.

To enhance your daily performance, put a small gold dot on the back of your hand or wear a gold wristband. These visual triggers are positive reminders for firing up your best attitude, putting forth your full effort, and maintaining a champion's outlook on life. The gold dot or wristband is forever linked to the "Think gold and never settle for silver" note and goes wherever you go.

Organize to synchronize. Many of us also need to make a commitment to get and stay more organized for greater efficiency and peace of mind. Do you have well-thought-out meals planned for each day, including balanced snacks? Do you have a packing plan when traveling to compete?

A good idea before traveling to a competition is to pack your kit a day early. Lay out your clothes, gear, an extra towel, balanced snacks (raisins, peanuts, and bananas), bottled water, and cash. Then charge your cell phone and iPod.

Keep in mind that other organizational changes in your life can boost your mood and performance. For example, maintain a clean, clutter-free bedroom, office, and sports locker; use color-coded file folders to sort all paperwork; recycle whatever you can; and keep a daily planner filled only with necessary reminders.

Periodically, spend 30 minutes organizing and cleaning your space to avoid major disorganization. Less clutter in your personal environment will decrease your stress level. For a boost, listen to music while you organize and clean. Don't stick with what you always play. Be adventurous: experiment with jazz, classical, hip-hop, classic rock, heavy metal, country, zydeco, and trance/techno music. You might surprise yourself by what music appeals to you in different situations.

POWER WITH PEOPLE

It was impossible to get a conversation going, everybody was talking too much.

—Yogi Berra

Social relationships can facilitate and/or impede your pursuit of excellence. As such, people skills can be just as important as athletic ability when it comes down to your enjoyment and success at sports. People skills pertain to an understanding of ourselves and others, talking and listening effectively, and building positive and productive relationships.

Team partners Misty May-Treanor and Kerri Walsh Jennings are the most decorated beach volleyball players ever. Recognizing the value of effective communication, they worked with a sports psychologist prior to the 2012 Olympics to further improve their communication with each other both on and off the court. In London, the dynamic duo went on to capture a record third-straight gold medal.

Whether you participate in an individual or team sport, good people skills are essential in helping you relate well and resolve conflict with others—coaches, teammates, media, athletic trainers, officials, opponents, family, and friends. Following are several points about developing good people skills:

Know your rights and entitlements. Do not let others violate your rights and entitlements. Do not tolerate verbal, physical, or sexual abuse. When someone's behavior violates your rights, let him or her know immediately instead of waiting to see if it happens again. Ideally, this should be stated explicitly. Likewise, you should respect the rights and entitlements of others.

Be present while listening. Give the other person your complete attention rather than planning your response or daydreaming. Maintain an attentive posture, make eye contact, and nod in agreement. Summarize what the other person is saying to convey your understanding. Good listening skills encourage the other person to talk.

Avoid mind reading. Ask the other person what he or she is thinking, feeling, or experiencing rather than telling them what you think he or she feels. Likewise, others shouldn't have to guess what you are thinking, feeling, or experiencing. Always keep the lines of communication open and respectful.

Discuss problems when they begin. Do not allow a problem with another person to fester. If needed, take a short break (or perhaps even a full day) to clear your head or calm down; then express how you feel and what you want corrected. This approach can resolve any misunderstanding quickly and get things back on track. Sulking about the issue does no good.

Criticize the behavior, not the person. Instead of saying, "You are such a . . . " which might be taken personally, a more productive approach would be to say, "When you said that about me in front of the team, I felt insulted. Was that your intent?" It is always better to be specific about the behavior you are challenging. Avoid generalizations such as "You never . . . " or "You always . . . "

Let fairness rule the day. Stop trying to be perfect or expecting others to be perfect. Look for a way to compromise when differences arise. In relationships with others, just ask yourself, "What is fair and reasonable to both parties in this situation?" The goal is to work together to find a solution that suits everyone. Avoid thinking in right-wrong, all-or-nothing, or good-bad dichotomies.

TEAMWORK: A SHARED DESTINY

A single arrow is easily broken, but not ten in a bundle.
—JAPANESE PROVERB

The Japanese story "Ten Jugs of Wine" exemplifies the difference between just being together on a team and working together as a real team. In the tale, ten old men decide to celebrate the New Year with a big crock of hot sake. Since none of them can provide for all, they each agree to bring one jug of wine for the large heating bowl. On the way to his wine cellar, each old man thinks, "My wine is too valuable to share! No one will know. It'll never show. It'll still be fine. I'll bring a jug of water instead of the wine."

And so when they gather with the jugs they brought, all ten men pour the contents of their jugs ceremoniously into the big bowl and then look sheepishly at one another as they heat and pour hot water for all.

Social loafing is the psychological term used to describe the phenomenon of the withholding behaviors demonstrated by the old men in the tale. Specifically, social loafing refers to the tendency of people to try less hard at a task when part of a group than when they are by themselves because of a diffusion of personal responsibility.

To be a gold medal teammate, remember the old men in "Ten Jugs of Wine." Instead of holding back, always bring the absolute best you have to offer from start to finish. Seize opportunities to assist your teammates and to aid your coaching staff with the day-to-day responsibilities of running the program. Do not water down your effort on or off the court by thinking that no one else will notice.

It is important to understand that a "rising tide lifts all boats." In other words, the more you give, the more your team will gain. And the more the team gains, the more you will receive in return, because everyone benefits from being part of a winning team. If you put forth your best effort, there are more intrinsic rewards (fun, purpose, and personal fulfillment) and extrinsic rewards (trophies, notice from scouts, and approval from others) to be had.

Good teammates help us to become the player we are meant to be. So always look for ways to bring out the best in one another and use one another for support as needed. "The teamwork is the most important thing, because when you have a group of guys who are playing for each other, playing hard and playing together, that trumps talent any day," says Chris Paul, all-star point guard for the NBA's Los Angeles Clippers.

A competitive tennis player recently shared the following with me: "One thing I have noticed is that in playing doubles tennis with higher-level players, we tend to focus on our spirit and positive state of mind when in a match. For example, saying, 'No worries on that shot, we're good. Stay loose.' Rather than what I notice with novices, where the doubles team is always commenting on their form or way to hit the ball. Even though we all know the next shot is not going to be like the last one!"

Championship teams often use terms like *chemistry, togetherness,* and *one heartbeat.* Trust is the foundation for the strong "we" feeling on championship teams. Everyone is pushing (or pulling) in the same direction. Keep battling, stay positive, and do it together as a team to break through poor starts or losing streaks. Always look for a way to help your team's cause. A team has a shared destiny, and as such, all behaviors must be for the benefit of the team and the greater good.

Think about these three self-reflection questions regarding your role as a teammate:

1. What am I doing that is hurting my team (e.g., complaining, gossiping)?

2. What am I *not* doing that is hurting my team (e.g., cheering for my teammates, accepting my role on the team)?

3. What are the specific action steps I will take to be a better teammate moving forward (e.g., hustling on every play, being more vocal on the field)?

LEAD BY CREED AND DEED

The strength of the group is the strength of the leaders.

—VINCE LOMBARDI

Leaders make a positive difference by helping others develop from good to gold medal. Every member of a team, not just the coaches or the designated captains, can and should be a leader. Everybody should look for opportunities for leadership in their own lives and think about ways they can make a positive impact on their teams.

Leadership responsibilities are taken very seriously within championship-caliber teams. While any team or athlete can have a winning attitude when the scoreboard is in their favor, a championship-caliber team understands that a winning attitude is most needed during tough times. Rather than pointing fingers or complaining, a championship-caliber team faces a loss or a lackluster performance with the attitude that "we're all going to get better and find a way to make this work."

John Wooden, the former UCLA men's basketball coach, led the Bruins to 10 NCAA basketball championships, as well as four undefeated seasons and an 88-game winning streak. Wooden was named Greatest Coach of the 20th Century by ESPN. He demonstrated a strong, positive leadership approach and defined success for himself and for those under his leadership in his informative book *Wooden on Leadership: How to Create a Winning Organization:*

> Before you can lead others, you must be able to lead yourself. Define success for those under your leadership as total commitment and effort to the team's welfare. Then show it yourself with your own effort and performance. Most of those you lead will do the same. Those who don't should be encouraged to look for a new team.

A strong, positive leadership style is crucial because destructive criticism and bullying does little to motivate people; in fact, it often causes people to shut down and stop trying. An affirmative approach will tend to produce relationships based on trust and mutual respect. How do you like to be treated by the powers that be? Most likely, the answer is positively and productively, rather than negatively and punitively. So make sure to treat others in the same fashion. Always be encouraging, up-front, and honest in your communication.

Here are 10 suggestions for becoming a champion leader:

1. Develop a vision for success and stay enthusiastic about pursuing it.

2. Great leaders invite feedback from others as opposed to blocking criticism. Always share credit and accept blame.

3. Have a strong sense of confidence and optimism about what you are doing. Stay calm and in control during a moment of crisis. Athletes need to know there is hope, and they will look to coaches and team leaders for cues.

4. Care, really care, about others. Take an interest in the person wearing the uniform, not just in that person's performance.

5. Respect and appreciate your own role, as well as the roles of others.

6. Realize that your impact goes beyond your performance; lead by example, on and off the field.

7. Hold everyone, including yourself, accountable for on-the-field and off-the-field behavior. Understand when providing a pat on the back or a friendly but firm reminder is most effective.

8. Learn to adapt to each situation, and use a style that suits the situation.

9. Share in all of the sacrifices and hardships of the team, never asking others to do what you are unwilling to do.

10. Do the right thing, even when the right thing is neither easy nor popular.

CHANGE IS THE NAME OF THE WINNING GAME

Unceasing change turns the wheel of life,
and so reality is shown in all its many forms.

—**BUDDHIST SAYING**

People tend not to like change, except for maybe a bus driver, a wet baby, or someone using a vending machine. But seriously, folks, major life changes or setbacks can represent a loss of routine, comfort, and our role in the family, team, organization, or community.

However, adjustments and transitions are things we can master.

We can move with changes by maintaining a flexible attitude. A flexible attitude is like a free-flowing stream. Now imagine a boulder in the water, stopping the flow: This is a rigid mind-set. Flow with changes by being curious about how you can navigate around (or even profit from) each obstruction instead of being discouraged by it.

Major changes encountered by athletes can include:

- Getting cut from tryouts
- Transition to college for a freshman student-athlete
- Losing one's starting position on a team
- An unexpected coaching change
- Dealing with a major injury
- A midseason trade to another team
- Retirement from competitive sports

Non-sports-related hardships can include:

- Parents' divorce
- A death in the family
- A relationship breakup
- Financial difficulties
- Roommate issues
- Geographic changes or homesickness
- Academic challenges
- A change in peer relationships

In the face of adversity, people are often racked with shame and guilt and stop taking care of themselves. Sometimes they direct their anger inward and become self-destructive by abusing alcohol or other drugs, procrastinating, or neglecting their personal appearance. They may fight with loved ones or friends in an attempt to drive others away when they are needed most.

When you get knocked down by disruptive change, get up right away. The answer for a champion is to "play it where it lies" by proactively dealing with the situation rather than avoiding it by pretending that you are immune to disappointment. Remember, the more you avoid, the more you will continue to avoid. Instead, be proactive rather than inactive in dealing with change.

Maximize positive adjustment by doing the right things, such as confiding in people close to you or a counselor when you feel emotionally stuck. Appreciate the people around you and ask for help from them when needed. Also, kick yourself back into gear when you are lying, hurting others, or being self-destructive.

Finally, be brilliant with the basics—because the fundamentals don't change.

The basics include:

- Adhering to your regular exercise or training program
- Sticking to your nutrition plan
- Maintaining a regular sleep schedule
- Taking time to relax and unwind
- Feeling what you need to feel
- Spending quality time with others
- Looking for opportunities to help others
- Updating your life goals and avoiding making any rash decisions

Even when you don't have a chance to be a starting player in one area of your life because of a major life change or setback, such as an illness, injury, or loss, you can still excel in other areas of your life by tapping into your talents.

As we've discussed in this chapter, becoming a champion requires that you go for the gold—battle against the best *and* your best—in all areas of your life and game, and not just for those few hours while you're running mile repeats on the track or churning out laps at the pool. The plan is to achieve daily acts of excellence in support of your ultimate dream goal. This is a key concept. Knowing this, ask yourself, "Am I chasing my dreams or just coasting along all day; am I striving for personal gold or settling for silver?"

CHAPTER TWO

MASTER THE
MENTAL SKILLS

You have to train your mind like you train your body.
—BRUCE JENNER

The science-based mental skills presented in this chapter are proven winners for helping athletes forge a champion's mindset in order to grasp their full capability. You will recognize some of the skills; your challenge will then be to master them. You will learn several powerful new skills that you can apply with ease to your game play. Adapt each mental skill to fit your particular needs and situation.

A mind-over-matter approach doesn't develop overnight. Follow the same learning process used to develop your physical skills: repetition (deliberate and daily mental practice) and reinforcement (feeling good about your efforts by saying things like "I'm gaining mental muscle."). To build mastery, stick to the improvement plan and try to focus on one or two mental skills multiple times each day to build a strong and fortified foundation. The mental skills are:

- **GOAL SETTING:** Think It, Then Ink It
- **MENTAL IMAGERY:** Visualize to Actualize
- **SELF-TALK:** Feed the Good Wolf

- **CONFIDENCE:** Flex Your Confidence Muscle
- **FOCUS:** A Champion Is a Now-ist
- **BREATH CONTROL:** Breathe Life into Your Performance
- **MENTAL TOUGHNESS:** Build Your Inner-Strength Bank Account
- **ANXIETY MANAGEMENT:** Go from Panicky to Pumped
- **ENJOYMENT:** Humor Is the Best Sports Medicine
- **BODY LANGUAGE:** Make a Golden Impression
- **INTENSITY:** Own Your Zone
- **PERSONAL AFFIRMATION WORKS:** Power Phrases for Becoming a Champion

GOAL SETTING: THINK IT, THEN INK IT

Set your goals high, and don't stop till you get there.
—BO JACKSON

What are your minor, short-term goals? What are your major, long-term goals? What is your ultimate dream goal for your sports career? Examples include making the varsity team, earning a college athletic scholarship, running a sub-three-hour marathon, and winning an Olympic gold medal. The important thing is that you define your objectives and clarify what it will take to get there. Then you can set in motion a plan to achieve these goals, making them a reality. To perform at a champion's level, know what your goals are and always keep them in focus.

There are several potential benefits of this goal setting.

Specifically, goals can increase your drive, your effort, and your will to strive and succeed. Goals can also increase your awareness of performance strengths and areas in need of improvement. They can light the path that will get you to where you want to end up. Your dream goal as an athlete, whatever it is, will serve as your guiding star. Then you can commit yourself to performing daily acts of excellence with your dream goal in mind.

Speed skater Dan Jansen won an Olympic gold medal in the 1000-meter race at the 1994 Lillehammer Winter Olympics, and he set eight world records over the course of his stellar career. He explained the importance of setting your goals high: "I don't think there's any such thing as setting your goals too high. The higher you set your goals, the more you are going to work—if you don't reach it, then it's okay, just as long as you set it and then give a hundred percent of yourself."

How great do you want to be? How much do you want to win? The key is to identify which goals are most important to you and then write them down and display them in a location where you can look to them for motivation, such as on your bedroom wall. Then set your sights on strategically taking your goals one at a time. That is, focus all of your energy, effort, and enthusiasm on executing your improvement plan, step by step, day by day.

The results you get are often based on the goals you set, so the goal-setting process is important. Make sure to enlist the assistance of a friend, teammate, coach, or mentor who can serve as an objective observer and provide encouragement. The following are five questions to ask yourself to evaluate each performance goal you set, whether the particular goal is for next week, this season, or your sports career:

- Is my goal *specific*?
- Is my goal *measurable*?

- Is my goal *positive*?
- Is my goal *inspiring*?
- Is my goal *displayed*?

Consider using a three-level goal system to determine your achievement levels at a training session, during the next competition, or in your upcoming season: 1) bronze, 2) silver, and 3) gold. In this system, bronze symbolizes a desired result that would be a good outcome based on a reasonable assessment of past performances and current capabilities. Silver refers to a significant improvement. Finally, gold is equivalent to achieving a best time or delivering a major performance breakthrough.

This system provides three levels of success rather than a narrowly defined target goal. Another advantage to this approach is that the top level has no limit, so you cannot sell yourself short by thinking small. Let's take a look at three creative examples of the three-level goal system in action across different sports:

1. A golfer with an average player handicap of 15 devises with his or her swing instructor an improvement plan and sets handicap index goals for the upcoming season: bronze: 15–13.5; silver: 13.4–11.5; gold: 11.4 or lower.

2. A sprinter with a recent time of 10.5 seconds in the 100 meters discusses with his track coach performance expectations for the upcoming meet: bronze: 10.6–10.5 seconds; silver: 10.49–10.4 seconds; gold: 10.39 seconds or faster.

3. A basketball player who makes 80 percent of her free throws attempts 100 shots after a regular team practice to work more on this area of her game. She gauges her performance as: bronze: 75–80 shots made; silver: 81–85 made; gold: 86 or more made.

Dr. Gary Hall Sr. swam for the United States on three Olympic teams (1968–1976), earning three medals. He set 10 world records during his spectacular career. At Indiana University, Hall won 13 Big Ten and 8 NCAA titles. He now operates the Race Club in the Florida Keys, a world-class training facility for swimmers of all ages and abilities. Hall shared with me his thoughts regarding goal setting:

> The two most important parts of setting goals are that you write them down and that you put them someplace where you can see them every day. I usually recommend the bathroom mirror or refrigerator door, two places I know you will always look. When I was 16 years old, training for my first Olympic Games, my coach wrote all of my goal times down on the top of the kickboard I was using every day in practice. I couldn't escape them, but the result, after executing the plan, was that I made the Olympic team.

MENTAL IMAGERY: VISUALIZE TO ACTUALIZE

See first with your mind, then with your eyes, and finally with your body.

—MASTER SWORDSMAN YAGYŪ MUNENORI (1571–1646)

Mental imagery, popularly referred to as visualization, is the process of using all your senses to help with learning and developing new sports skills and strategies as well as visualizing success. Imagining optimal performance is accomplished by creating or re-creating the whole or part of a sporting event. This type of mental rehearsal can be likened to learning a physical skill: The more you deliberately practice, the better you will become at the actual task. Thus, imagery goes far beyond daydreaming. As with physical practice, mental practice requires structure and discipline for you to reap its full benefit.

Scores of experimental studies have explored the effects of mental imagery on physical performance. In 1983, Drs. Deborah Feltz and Daniel Landers, prominent researchers in sports psychology, completed a thorough review of mental practice literature and confirmed the benefits of using imagery for performance enhancement. Their findings demonstrated that imagery is one of the most powerful performance weapons we have in our mental arsenal.

Although imagery will not guarantee that you will always reach best times or win the game, mastery of this mental skill will increase the probability of success in sports. Specifically, imagery works to enhance one's performance by sharpening the mental blueprint and strengthening the muscle memory for the physical purpose at hand. This is why imagery is used by virtually all Olympic athletes as a critical part of their training regimens. Imagery can be used to prepare for all athletic performances, regardless of the motor skills involved.

The brain does not always differentiate between real and vividly imaged experiences because the same systems in the brain are deployed for both types of experience. For example, a common nightmare is that of being pursued. The dreamer is safely at home in bed yet awakens frightened—breathing fast, heart pounding. It's all in the mind, yet the dreamer experiences the physical sensations that would accompany a real, waking pursuit.

Dr. Henry "Hap" Davis, a neuroscience researcher and sports psychologist, has studied brain function in elite athletes, using magnetic resonance imaging (MRI) to monitor their neural activity. A 2008 study examined elite athletes watching videos of personal success or failure. Athletes reexperiencing a successful performance showed a greater increase in neural activity in the right premotor cortex, an area of the brain that plans actions, than those reexperiencing a failure.

Visualize positive performances and picture the ideal steps for achieving the successful result. Create a crystal clear mental image and powerful physical feeling of what you want to accomplish. Include the sights, sounds, smells, tactile impressions, and powerful emotions that accompany the total performance experience while in your virtual arena. The clarity and controllability of your images will improve with practice.

When visualizing, strive to experience the action in 3-D from the first-person point of view (through your own eyes), as opposed to a third-person point of view (through the eyes of spectator). The aim during imagery rehearsal is to "see it, feel it, and enjoy it" (SFE). You experience yourself having achieved your goal through your own eyes, rather than watching yourself from the outside.

Here are three key ingredients for successful imagery rehearsal:

1. Vividly *see* yourself performing successfully.

2. Deeply *feel* yourself performing masterfully.

3. Thoroughly *enjoy* seeing and feeling yourself winning.

A veteran NFL punter with whom I worked has developed a form of weight training for the mind. For 10 minutes every other day, he gets in a relaxed state through deep breathing, and then he "sees and feels" himself executing successful punts in a variety of game situations and weather conditions (using best-, average-, and worst-case scenarios). He uses imagery as a mental walk-through to preexperience flawless performances and expertly handling any adversity that might occur. He was also familiar with the stadiums on his schedule, so he was able to picture himself there playing in his next game.

Canadian Duff Gibson, the gold medalist in the skeleton at the

Turin Winter Olympics in 2006, described to me how he used visualization to attain peak performance:

> In the sport of skeleton, visualization is key. When you're
> sliding down an ice run faster than a car goes down the
> freeway, to be successful and for your own safety, you
> need to be completely focused and in the moment. Visu-
> alization, like anything, gets better with practice, and
> ultimately I was able to use the skill to prepare for the
> sequence of turns on a given track as well as to gain my
> focus for what I was about to do. Through visualization
> I also trained myself to be very relaxed on the sled,
> which is critical to generating speed.

Briton Steve Backley, the onetime world record holder for javelin
throwing, won four gold medals at the European Championships,
three Commonwealth Games gold medals, two silvers and a bronze
at the Olympic Games, and two silvers at the World Championships. I was curious which mental skill Steve found most helpful to
his performance throughout his remarkable career. He explained:

> I find it hard to distinguish one out of all the mental
> skills, as there were various that were pertinent at differ-
> ent times. And I guess that in itself is one of the more
> important ones—knowing what to do and when. Having
> said that, I'd have to single out the ability to visualize. To
> be able to preempt the future by building high-definition
> videos in your mind's eye of exactly what it is you are
> trying to achieve. I had the unfortunate incident of
> injury in the later stages of a buildup to an Olympic
> Games which gave me the tremendous opportunity to
> test this principle of preparation to the maximum. I basi-
> cally did all of my late prep for the '96 Games using this

kind of visualization. That is, instead of training, I saw it in my mind's eye. Lots more detail to this, but the result was one of my best-ever performances and a silver medal that I will cherish more than any gold.

Mentally practice two or three times each week for about 10 to 15 minutes per rehearsal. Select a specific sports skill to further develop, or work your way though different scenarios, incorporating various game-ending situations. Examples include meeting your marathon goal time, striking out the side in the bottom of the ninth, or making the game-winning shot as the final buzzer is sounding.

Mental practice sessions that are shorter in length are also beneficial. Good times include during any downtime in your schedule, the night before a competition, as an element of your pregame routine, and especially as part of a preshot routine. For example, consider a golfer during tournament play. The player should always attempt to see and feel a successful shot before actually swinging the club.

Let's conclude our discussion with a mental practice exercise. Sit up in a chair with your back straight (rather than lying down on a bed or on the floor, as this can make you sleepy). Let your eyes close and become aware of your breathing. Take a few slow, deep breaths (in through the nose and out through the mouth) to clear your mind and relax your body. Select a specific skill in your sport, such as a free throw in basketball or a kick serve in tennis.

Begin by creating a mental picture of your environment, progressively including all of the sights and sounds. Pay particular attention to the physical sensations in your body, such as the spring in your ankles and knees, whether your breathing is heavy or relaxed, the weight of the racquet or ball in your hand, and the texture of the ball as you spin or bounce it.

As you mentally start to go through your preshot or pre-serve routine—for instance, bouncing the ball three times, taking a deep breath, and seeing your target—inhale deeply and let the breath move through your body. Now fully *see*, *feel*, and *enjoy* executing this skill throughout each moment of the movement. Maintain full attention throughout the entire activity and complete the routine by sinking the basket with a swish or serving an ace down the line.

Challenge yourself to do this exercise successfully three times in a row with full focus and a positive result. If you visualize missing the basket or hitting the ball into the net or if you lose focus, keep repeating the process until you can visualize yourself doing it right straight through. This will further anchor your physical self to a gold medal performance.

SELF-TALK:
FEED THE GOOD WOLF

What you're thinking, what shape your mind is in,
is what makes the biggest difference of all.

—WILLIE MAYS

There is an old Cherokee legend known as the tale of the two wolves. A grandfather explains to his warrior grandson that there are two wolves within each of us: One wolf is positive and beneficial, while the other wolf is negative and destructive. These two wolves fight for control over us. The grandson is curious and asks, "Which wolf will win?" The grandfather replies, "The one you feed."

If thoughts determine feelings, then feelings influence performance. That being the solid-gold truth, learn to think more positively about yourself and your game. That is, monitor what you tell yourself and always feed the good wolf, not the bad wolf! This is one of the most important life lessons you can ever learn. Understanding that this choice is yours alone is very empowering and important.

The first step in feeding the good wolf is learning to identify your own negative and self-defeating thoughts. Typical negative thoughts an athlete can have include "I suck at this," "I'm not good enough," or, "I don't belong on the team." We all have these thoughts at times, so take a moment right now and identify some common negative thoughts about your athletic capabilities that run through your mind while you are at practice or in a game.

Now take the second step in feeding the good wolf and challenge these self-critical thoughts (such as "I'm not cut out for this") with encouraging statements (such as "Bring it on now!"). Mentally beating on yourself does you no good. Instead, gain clear control of your thinking processes. Repeat these two winning steps to build mental muscle, improve your mood, and advance your athletic performance.

When the bad wolf (or Big Bad Wolf!) rears its ugly head during competition, stop it in its tracks. Self-talk (i.e., saying words or short phrases to oneself) should be positive: "I've just made a penalty. I'm getting anxious, I'm dwelling on it. Stop. Breathe. I'm pressing the reset button and deleting that memory from my mind. It's over. I'm going to take a fresh, confident look at the next play in front of me." In quick-reaction sports like basketball and soccer, simply shout to yourself, "Next play!"

In a recent meta-analysis of 32 previously published sports psychology studies, Dr. Antonis Hatzigeorgiadis and his colleagues at the University of Thessaly in Greece confirmed that self-talk can produce significant improvements in sports performance. Their article was published in the July 2011 edition of *Perspectives on Psychological Science*. Hatzigeorgiadis says, "The mind guides action. If we succeed in regulating our thoughts, then this will help our behavior."

Additionally, the researchers looked at various uses of self-talk for different tasks. For tasks requiring fine motor skills, such as golf, instructional self-talk (e.g., "Do a full shoulder turn") was found to be more effective than motivational self-talk (e.g., "I'm the best"). Conversely, motivational self-talk was found to be more effective for tasks requiring strength or endurance, such as running or cycling. Self-talk can be more valuable for novel tasks than for well-learned tasks, and both beginning and experienced athletes can benefit from this technique.

Although you probably cannot eliminate all of your negative thoughts, you do have the power to challenge these thoughts and replace them with more positive and useful ideas. As we will further discuss, the ultimate goal in the moment of action is to transcend conscious thinking so that you are fully *experiencing* your performance in the moment (i.e., you are in a flow or zone state). Seek to improve the quality of your thoughts and to quiet the mind. To perform at a champion's level, always feed the good wolf in you!

CONFIDENCE: FLEX YOUR CONFIDENCE MUSCLE

Every strike brings me closer to the next home run.

—BABE RUTH

Sports psychology studies and anecdotal reports from winning athletes confirm that confidence is crucial for athletic success. Specifically, self-confidence is a strong belief in one's skills, preparation, and abilities. Confidence in tough situations is the mark of a great player, according to legendary tennis player John McEnroe. In order to be successful, you must believe that you can be successful.

True confidence is a hard-earned trait. Golf legend Jack Nicklaus built his confidence through proper preparation, particularly for the four major tournaments a year. He won a record 18 professional major championships, but he also had 19 runner-up finishes and 9 third-place finishes—in an astonishing 46 major tournaments he was still in the top three on Sunday.

In an interview after winning a major championship, Nicklaus remarked, "As long as I'm prepared, I always expect to win." Demonstrated performance (reflecting on previous successes and high points) and proper preparation (in terms of quality and quantity) are the two primary ways to gain confidence for competition.

To paraphrase sprinter Maurice Greene, a onetime world record holder in the 100 meters, train like you are No. 2 (train your talent), but compete like you are No. 1 (trust your talent). On game day, play confidently by emphasizing your skills and strengths, drawing from past successes, and appreciating the encouragement from your coaches and teammates. Emphasize your strengths and your opponents' weaknesses—not vice versa.

Remember, then, to identify similarities between the challenge at the moment and previous situations in which you have excelled or surpassed your expectations. Tell yourself, "I've done this before and I can do it now." Focus on your performance, not on unwanted outcomes.

To perform at a champion's level, you must understand the importance of a long-term memory for success and a short-term memory (selective amnesia) for failure. Every athlete fails, but champions do not dwell on their failures. Instead, they focus on the positive experiences and keep confidently moving forward.

Middle-distance runner Noureddine Morceli of Algeria trusted his talent, no matter how tough his competitors appeared to be. Morceli, the 1996 Atlanta Olympic gold medalist in the 1500 meters, said in a Nike advertisement, "When I race, my mind is full of doubts—who will finish second, who will finish third?"

Complacency is often the culprit when an athlete or team blows a big lead or loses to an "inferior" opponent (who obviously did not see themselves as inferior). Extremely high confidence is never the problem, provided that you are continuously working hard and intelligently in training to become the best athlete you can be and you have an undying will to win during competition: You can hate to lose, but don't be afraid to lose. Confidence without complacency keeps you on target when you are playing well and winning.

Several self-reflection questions are included here, based on the pioneering work on the topic of self-efficacy (a specific strength of belief) by Stanford psychologist Dr. Albert Bandura beginning in the mid-1970s. These questions are designed to raise your confidence as you review accomplishments, recall positive feedback, resolve to mirror and model your athletic heroes, and listen to reminders of your capabilities.

1. What has been the biggest challenge to date that you have overcome in your sport, and how did you overcome it? Examples include bouncing back from a major injury, busting out of a slump, or completing your first marathon or triathlon.

2. Describe your greatest sports performance to date. Spend a few minutes reliving the glory and magic moments from this performance in vivid color. What helped you make it over the top? What were your thoughts and feelings during the game, match, or race?

3. What are three of your signature strengths or attributes as an athlete? Be honest, but don't be modest in answering this question. Examples include work ethic, mental toughness, and focus.

4. What are three compliments you have received from others that made you feel really good about yourself? Examples include a coach describing you as the hardest worker on the team, opponents saying you were their toughest competition, or a teammate calling you a warrior on the field.

5. Who in your life wouldn't be surprised to see you overcome the challenge before you now and/or accomplish your biggest goal? Examples include your mother, father, sibling, grandparent, coach, teammate, or friend.

6. What are three awards or accomplishments that you have earned? Examples include an individual or team trophy, an athletic scholarship, or a personal best in your performance.

7. Identify three athletic heroes or role models (currently or from childhood) that you can mirror or mimic when you need a confidence boost during a challenging situation. Perhaps your favorite player battled through on-the-field adversity by showing tremendous resolve when he or she played. Remember, if you can spot the greatness in others, then you already have some of that greatness in yourself.

FOCUS: A CHAMPION IS A NOW-IST

The time is now, the place is here.
—DAN MILLMAN

Focus, or selective attention, is your dedication to the task at hand to the exclusion of all else. In sports, focus requires screening out useless information (fog) to concentrate on the target, such as the bull's-eye in archery or the flag in golf. The preferred sequence is to lock on the immediate target, disregard distractions, and prevail.

Michael Phelps, history's most decorated Olympian with 22 total medals (including 18 golds!), put his headphones on when he went to the pool to get into his own little world. The only thing that mattered to him was swimming his best. Phelps was able to reach a level of focus and drive never seen before in his sport. He discussed the significance of focus in his book *No Limits: The Will to Succeed*:

> When I'm focused, there is not one single thing, person, anything that can stand in my way of my doing something. There is not. If I want something bad enough, I feel I'm gonna get there.

Let's say for each moment an athlete has $100 worth of focus, and he or she can spend it in any manner. A dollar spent on an internal and/or external distraction during performance is a dollar wasted because you are not getting the full value from your abilities. Where is your focus when you compete? Are you caught up with distractions or do you stay on target?

Spend all of your focus dollars efficiently—on the process of performance instead of on any potential distractions. For instance, a goalie in soccer should fully focus on playing moment to moment by tracking the ball with her eyes instead of dwelling on having just allowed a goal and glancing at the bleachers or at the other team's bench to gauge reactions.

Focus keeps distractions at bay. Distractions come in two forms: external and internal.

COMMON EXTERNAL DISTRACTIONS

- Crowd noise
- Photo flashes

- Public announcements
- Scoreboard
- Shadows
- Trash talk by opponents
- Inclement weather (hot/cold, wind/rain)

COMMON INTERNAL DISTRACTIONS

- Hunger
- Thirst
- Fatigue
- Soreness
- Subversive thoughts
- Negative emotions
- Boredom

An important realization to accept is that something is a distraction only if you consider it a distraction. Simply look away. Ignore noises (even from your Big Bad Wolf). Focus on your breathing and your body. Be aware of your easing grip on the golf club, hockey stick, baseball/softball bat, or tennis racquet. In sum, trust your five senses to "feel the now" and stay in the moment. That is, always strive to be a now-ist.

Your thought process must be simplified and concerned only with what is happening now to win or reach your peak performance in sports. Always stay fully focused in the moment on the field of play. Thoughts about the past and future are fog, and thoughts about the present—the here and now—are clear skies.

Being present in the moment empowers you to respond with alertness, curiosity, and skill to whatever comes your way. Nothing else matters; your focus is on putting your purpose in the cross hairs and taking your best shot. When you are clearly focused on the present task, then you free yourself to thoroughly enjoy the experience.

Full presence produces seamless fusion—you become your performance. Otherwise, you are always one step behind what you are doing because you are judging what is happening and are not fully in the moment. A mind in the moment is not self-conscious or concerned about what opponents or spectators are thinking or doing.

Chris Sharma, one of the world's best rock climbers, says he gets so focused when he climbs hard routes that he *completely* loses himself. He channels all his energy directly into what he is doing in the moment of the climb. In the same way, get out of yourself and get *into* your performance no matter what that performance may be.

Your mind will continually drift off or zone out as you decide to focus on the moment's challenges. Keep reminding yourself to "Be all here!" or shout, "Now!" when you discover that your mind has wandered back to the past or forward to the future. Extraneous thoughts should not be given a lot of airtime.

Through increased self-awareness and mental discipline, you can train your mind to remain squarely in the present. The present is always the present, and it's all that ever is; the past and future exist only in your imagination.

BREATH CONTROL: BREATHE LIFE INTO YOUR PERFORMANCE

Your breathing determines whether you are at your best or whether you are at a disadvantage.

—CAROLA SPEADS, AUTHOR AND TEACHER OF BREATHING PRACTICES

To perform at a champion's level, breathe deeply and rhythmically to maintain peak energy levels. Proper breathing works in tandem with being a Now-ist (i.e., living fully in the moment). Expand the belly during inhalation and relax the belly during exhalation. Let your shoulders drop and jaw relax as you exhale. Give it a try right now. Draw in a deep breath and let it out slowly.

Your breathing can become shallow when you feel angry or anxious. When this occurs, oxygen intake diminishes and muscle tension increases. So make sure to take a deep breath in tough situations. Simply prolonging exhalation, regardless of inhalation length, promotes the relaxation response. Proper breathing helps expel the stress and tension from your system and brings you back into the present.

Many top coaches and elite athletes practice deep breathing for mental training. For example, consider Phil Jackson, who won a record 11 NBA titles as the head coach of the Chicago Bulls and the Los Angeles Lakers. He also played on two NBA champion New York Knicks teams. As a coach, he emphasized to his players the significance of deep and mindful breathing, especially before games and between quarters.

Check in with your breathing throughout the day. Are you

breathing from the belly or from the chest? Is the breath deep or shallow? There are three simple steps to taking a deep, centering breath:

1. Breathe in through the nose for a count of one, two, three, four, and five.

2. Hold for one and two.

3. Breathe out through the mouth for a count of one, two, three, four, five, six, seven, and eight.

Mentally count to five for the in-breath, count to two as you hold the breath, and count to eight for the out-breath. Take your time with this 15-second breathing intervention and repeat the steps for four cycles (your 1-minute breath workout) or as many times as desired. Do this exercise when you observe that you are getting tense, feeling down or stuck in a repetitive negative-thinking cycle. Breathing in this manner will help you to slow your heart rate, calm your thoughts, and find inner stillness in the moment.

Learn how to sit quietly without doing anything other than fol-lowing the breath. Listening to the breath is helpful because it feels more active. Listening to the breath works well for those who are often distracted or feel the need to be doing something.

Extraneous thoughts fog up your focus. Your mind becomes more powerful as it becomes quieter and clearer. So breathe deeply and mindfully throughout your day. Also, when you are not think-ing about the future, it's difficult to fear it. Fear is the enemy of effective action!

MENTAL TOUGHNESS: BUILD YOUR INNER-STRENGTH BANK ACCOUNT

The most important attribute a player
must have is mental toughness.

—MIA HAMM

Mental toughness does not entail clenching your teeth, trying harder, thinking more, straining your eyes to focus, or having someone scream "Be tough!" at you. Mental toughness is the ability to remain positive and proactive in the most adverse of circumstances.

Mental toughness is built on doing the thing that is hard over and over again, especially when you don't feel like doing it. Push through on your down days when you are not feeling your best. Distraction, discomfort, and difficulties are no match for the champion.

This dogged determination requires keeping your feet moving forward through inconveniences, substantial discomfort, and insecurities to reach your top goal. When you want something really badly, don't give up until you've got it.

Mental toughness can be demonstrated at a particular moment in time or over the long term, as in your overall career success. Doing the thing that is hard over and over again is like depositing money in your inner-strength bank account.

Distance runner Emil Zátopek is one example of an athlete who used mental toughness in his training to reach the top. He won three gold medals in the 1952 Helsinki Olympics, including victory in the first marathon he ever entered. Overall, Zátopek won a total of five Olympic medals: four golds and one silver.

Dubbed the "Czech Locomotive," Zátopek said, "If one can stick to the training throughout the many long years, then willpower is no longer a problem. It's raining? That doesn't matter. I am tired? That's beside the point. It's simply that I just have to."

Around the time Zátopek was tearing up the track, Billy Mills was living in poverty in Pine Ridge, South Dakota. He was orphaned at the age of 12 and was raised on an Indian reservation rife with alcoholism. He turned to athletics for a positive outlet and eventually took up running.

Mills made the U.S. Olympic track-and-field team for the 1964 Tokyo Olympics. He was an afterthought in the 10,000-meter race—his qualifying time was almost a full minute slower than the favorites.

However, the fiercely resilient Mills overcame a lack of international experience, a wicked shove and elbow on the last lap by the favorite Ron Clarke, and being boxed in on the final turn. Nevertheless, he blasted down the final stretch and won the gold in record time.

In the 2007 NFL divisional playoff game between the Green Bay Packers and Seattle Seahawks, Packers running back Ryan Grant fumbled twice in the first 4 minutes and his team fell behind 14–0. He told himself, "It happened, that sucks, gotta move on."

A champion knows that thoughts cause feelings, and feelings affect performance. Rather than retreating into a shell, Grant gave himself a pep talk and gained 201 yards and scored three touchdowns to help lead his team to an impressive come-from-behind 42–20 victory. He was able to "fumble and forget" so he could get back to work.

It is always better to acknowledge and accept whatever happens. Then let it go and focus forward with complete confidence. Grant's attitude was that he needed to keep his head in the game because there was a lot of football left to be played. Always remember, whether in training or competition, tough times require mentally tough responses.

ANXIETY MANAGEMENT: GO FROM PANICKY TO PUMPED

Get your butterflies to fly in formation.
—SPORTS PSYCHOLOGY ADAGE

Most athletes feel anxious before and during competition. They accept performance anxiety as perfectly normal and let it sharpen their focus. This anxiety or excitement is proof that they, and you, care about performance and outcomes. Of course, too much anxiety is uncomfortable and interferes with performance.

A moderate level of anxiety or excitement is necessary for optimal performance. In sports, panic is typically an extreme form of performance anxiety. A panic response is thus an exaggerated mind-body reaction—a false alarm—that can be diffused or redirected. Our instinctive responses to panic are always counterproductive, such as fleeing, isolating ourselves, trying too hard to relax, or beating ourselves up mentally.

If you have a high level of performance anxiety, then you've learned a sequence of responses. Once you trigger the sequence, it is difficult to stop the dominoes from falling. Your priority, then, is to stop the sequence early. What you truly fear, if you are willing to admit it, is *embarrassment* that you will fail to perform in the moment and because of that must suffer the consequences of anxiety and panic.

Panic always eventually leads to the subsiding of anxiety. The cliché of a "wolf in sheep's clothing" in sports describes a dangerous player pretending to be inept. Remember, then, that panic is a harmless experience that exists only in your mind, and by extension, in your body. Panicking is not going crazy, but rather the manifestation of fear of a terrible outcome.

Several tactics follow to help you triumph over performance anxiety so that you can fully enjoy sports and perform at your best. These tactics are not designed to eliminate intense feelings but to redirect them toward a positive outcome.

Be well prepared. The more prepared you are for competition, the less you will fear it. Nothing helps build confidence more than knowing that you are ready for the challenge at hand. Proper preparation comes from paying close attention to feedback from coaches, studying the playbook or game film, and practicing conscientiously. Without this kind of preparation, performance anxiety is more likely to occur. Before the game, always remind yourself that you have honestly prepared as best as possible.

Nerves are natural. It's normal to be anxious, so don't concern yourself with what other athletes might be thinking or how well they seem to be doing. We often don't suspect that others are overcome with or overwhelmed by anxiety. No matter how calm your opponents may appear, they are likely experiencing the same level of anxiety—or more so—than you are.

Ally with the anxiety. Do not attempt to rid yourself of the anxiety; instead, channel it into performing well, and talk to yourself about trying to use your anxiety instead of trying to avoid it. Tell yourself, "My body is preparing itself to perform," and "I've done well before, and I can do it again now."

Breathe evenly and deeply. Take a series of deep breaths to calm your nerves. Good breathing reduces anxiety by clearing your mind of fog and by reducing physical tension. Simply prolonging exhalation, regardless of inhalation length, promotes the relaxation response, so regulate each breath with a deep inhalation and a full exhalation.

Get creative and use your imagination. For instance, give the anxious feeling an imaginary form (such as a sparkler or firecracker) and then place it in an imaginary safe place or container that will protect you from it. Understand that you are bigger and more powerful than this anxious feeling.

Stay in the here and now. Monitor negative "futurizing" and worrisome thoughts about winning or losing. The results and outcomes can wait while you remain focused on playing each play to the best of your ability, one by one, until the final whistle.

Stay on a positive thought channel. Flip the switch from negative to positive self-talk when you are emotionally spiraling down. Try to talk sense to yourself (feed the good wolf) instead of letting your fear run wild (feeding the bad wolf). Remind yourself, "Even though I am feeling anxious and uncomfortable right now, I can still play well and reach my goals."

Take yourself lightly. A competition is an opportunity to test your fitness, challenge the competition, and demonstrate how hard you've worked. You are not your game. Take what you are doing seriously, but learn to take yourself lightly. Always remember that sport is what you do and not who you are. Smile. Laugh. Have a good time. Ask yourself, "What's the worst thing that can really happen?" If the worst does happen, ask, "What can I do to cope?"

To move forward rather than becoming overwhelmed and backing up when anxiety strikes, make use of the strategies presented so you can channel anxiety into commitment to taking the next step. Remember that FEAR means to "Face Everything and Respond." To perform at a champion's level, let the butterflies fly in formation!

ENJOYMENT:
HUMOR IS THE BEST
SPORTS MEDICINE

Every survival kit should include a sense of humor.

—ANONYMOUS

Imagine the following scenario: You are the quarterback and your team is down 16–13 in the Super Bowl. The ball is on your 8-yard line and only 3 minutes 10 seconds remain on the clock. What do you say to your team in the huddle? This is the exact same situation that Joe Montana faced when his San Francisco 49ers played the Cincinnati Bengals in Super Bowl XXIII. He decided to alleviate stress and pressure as he pointed to the stadium crowd and said, "Hey, isn't that John Candy?"

For the remainder of the game, the 49ers proceeded to drive down the field for the winning touchdown, scoring with 34 seconds left to spare. It was clutch performances such as this that earned Montana the nickname "Joe Cool."

Another classic story about the necessity of humor in sports comes from professional tennis. Vitas Gerulaitis, one of the top male tennis players during the late 1970s and early 1980s, was ranked as high as number three in the world in 1978. Despite his ability, Gerulaitis had been beaten by Jimmy Connors a hard-to-swallow 16 times straight. After finally breaking through and defeating Connors in 1980, Gerulaitis declared, "And let that be a lesson to you all. Nobody beats Vitas Gerulaitis seventeen times in a row!" Clearly, Gerulaitis was able to maintain his confidence and laugh at the situation despite the losing streak against Connors.

Steffi Graf, renowned as one of the greatest female tennis

players in history, had a memorable moment during the 1996 Wimbledon semifinal against Kimiko Date.

During a tense part of the match, as she readied to serve, a spectator yelled out, "Steffi, will you marry me?" As the fans in the stadium burst into laughter, she smiled and yelled back, "How much money do you have?"

While her disposition was typically stoic, her playful response to the comical court proposal helped lighten the mood and release tension. Graf went on to win the match and then defeat Arantxa Sánchez Vicario for the title.

There's great truth in the popular phrase that "humor is the best medicine," or in saying that laughter is "internal jogging."A good sense of humor is important for peak performance, as well as health and happiness. Humor is often misinterpreted in sports as being a sign of distraction or not caring about one's performance. However, finding humor in difficult situations is often the best way to reduce unnecessary stress and increase motivation.

A touch of humor at the right time keeps things from becoming too tense. This may help to explain why military personnel, police officers, and firefighters are often described as having sufficiently developed senses of humor. Lieutenant General Chesty Puller, the most decorated marine in U.S. history, told his soldiers, "We're surrounded. That simplifies the problem!" A good laugh can reduce stress, boost performance, and improve mood.

A coach can lighten the mood and alleviate tension for his or her team by periodically incorporating fun practice games or activities. A swim coach, for instance, might surprise his or her team by having them finish practice with a game of water polo. A baseball team can play a game of kickball, while a soccer team can gather together for a little Wiffle ball. Throwing a football or a Frisbee around can also be a lot of fun.

During the 2013 college basketball season, after the reigning national champion Kentucky Wildcats lost their best player for the season with a torn ACL and a subsequent 30-point blowout loss at Tennessee, Coach John Calipari organized a game of dodge ball between staff and players to have a good time and take their minds off basketball. The Wildcats returned to their winning ways by toppling Vanderbilt the very next night.

What does an umpire say to begin a game of baseball? He or she shouts, "Play ball!" not "Work ball!" There is a simple and straightforward reason behind this fact. Sports are meant to be played and enjoyed, enhanced by fun and humor whenever possible. There is no doubt that this shared laughter can form instant and long-lasting bonds among teammates, as long as stories and jokes are not mean-spirited.

Here are some practical strategies for enhancing your sense of humor and finding greater enjoyment in your sport:

- Have teammates with whom you share jokes and funny stories.

- Watch humor—comedy movies, TV sitcoms, and stand-up comedians.

- Read humor—comics, funny books, satirical websites (e.g., the Onion).

- Utilize props—flush away bad performances with a miniature toy toilet that you keep in your locker.

Bottom line: The more enjoyable the experience, the better your performance will be. Skip Bertman coached the LSU Tigers baseball team to five NCAA titles from 1984 to 2001. He said, "It is critical to not let the pressure of competition become greater than the pleasure of competition." To move forward, seek out things to love about your game and reasons to enjoy it.

BODY LANGUAGE: MAKE A GOLDEN IMPRESSION

Warriors don't slouch into battle.

—ANONYMOUS

Body language is nonverbal communication consisting of postures, gestures, facial expressions, and eye movements. Body language is a two-way process: Your own body language reveals your thoughts and feelings to others; and other people's body language reveals their thoughts and feelings to you. The body language of athletes and coaches is easy to pick up on while watching a sporting event, and it is usually representative of who is winning or losing at the moment. On game day, what is your body language saying? What image do you want to project?

Are you feeling intimidated before playing a top-ranked opponent? If so, are you taking a few moments to go through a few simple motions that can improve your readiness? According to recent research by psychologists Dana Carney, Amy Cuddy, and Andy Yap, simply holding one's body in open, expansive (versus closed, contractive) postures for only a couple of minutes can produce meaningful elevations in testosterone, decreases in cortisol, and increased feelings of power and tolerance for risk when it is needed. Thus, high-power postures can generate powerful responses. As such, looking like a winner will help you play like a winner.

Body language can be positive or negative:

POSITIVE/UPBEAT BODY LANGUAGE

- Smiling
- Chin up

- Shoulders back/chest out

- Standing tall

- Walking strong

NEGATIVE/GLUM BODY LANGUAGE

- Frowning

- Shaking your head

- Eyes downcast

- Shoulders hunched

- Dragging your feet

Adopt the pose of a supremely confident athlete for the duration of your practices and games. Acting this way will help you stay in a winning frame of mind, regardless of the score or situation. When you are gassed at practice, stand tall and walk strong. When you are playing an undefeated team, show your swagger.

Are you prone to making I-just-drank-some-expired-milk facial expressions or showing negative body language after missing a shot on goal or making an error in the field? To perform at a champion's level (and to be a good teammate), keep a positive demeanor and attitude rather than pouting or moping. Your body language will send the right message to the opposition: You can't be mentally beaten or fazed—no matter what happens.

Just smile, you'll feel better. Imagine that one day you are feeling down—perhaps something did not go as well as expected. But there isn't time for exploring your feelings because you have to start mentally preparing for that night's game. How can you quickly get into a better mood? Perhaps you've heard the expression "Just smile, you'll feel better." Does the act of smiling itself really make you feel better?

Findings from a 1988 research study by psychologist Fritz Strack and his colleagues revealed that simply creating a smile by clenching a pen lightly between the teeth will almost immediately make people feel happier about what it is they are doing. So keep this discovery in mind when you need a quick boost in mood. Do not simply drag a down mood into your performance. Put a big confident smile on your face instead!

Always give your BEST. Psychologist John Clabby has coined a handy acronym for giving one's BEST—"Body Language, Eye Contact, Speech, and Tone of Voice." Strive to always give your absolute BEST: body language (strong, not slumped), eye contact (focused, not wandering), speech (assertive, not passive), and tone of voice (self-assured, not soft). Strive to sharpen these four aspects of your communication further. Working on them at practices will make them automatic in competition.

Dress for success. As a final point, don't overlook your appearance. Wear your uniform with pride. Deion Sanders excelled at the highest level in both football and baseball. During his 14-year NFL career, Sanders was a perennial All-Pro, and he won the Super Bowl with both the San Francisco 49ers and the Dallas Cowboys. In the 1989 season, he scored a touchdown for the Atlanta Falcons and hit a home run for the New York Yankees during the same week. He says, "If you look good, you feel good. And if you feel good, you play good. If you play good, they pay good."

At the end of the day, all sports and competition are a combination of chance, practice, skill, and competitiveness. While not all of these components are in your control, each performance can be elevated by a strong mental attitude. Techniques to build your mental strength in practices and games include utilizing the BEST routine, valuing your appearance, and putting on a smile to push you past your perceived physical limitations.

INTENSITY:
OWN YOUR ZONE

Don't get psyched up, get psyched right.

—ANONYMOUS

When athletes are "flowing" or "in the zone," they are maintaining a certain intensity level while being mindful of the moment, which helps them achieve their peak performance. Since a direct relationship exists between performance quality and intensity level, your performance may be poorer when your intensity level is too low (you feel tired or disinterested) or too high (you feel wired or overexcited). For example, if your intensity level is low when competing against an unranked opponent, your play might be sloppy. Conversely, if your intensity level is high when competing against the top-ranked opponent, you may play at too hurried a pace.

To get in the zone, each athlete has an optimal intensity level for peak performance, depending on their sport. For example, golf is a game of calm, serenity, and narrow focus. American football, on the other hand, is associated with passion, emotion, and excitement. Yet a golfer might need to increase his or her intensity level to blast a long drive, while a quarterback might need to decrease his intensity level for precision passing.

To find your zone—or "golden median"—so you can perform at your best, you must learn to throttle up or throttle down to find the ideal intensity for each situation. A biathlete, for instance, must be able to throttle up for cross-country skiing and then throttle down to sharpen his or her results on the rifle range. Consider the following strategies to increase or decrease your intensity levels to meet the demands of the situation.

Throttle up. Imagine you need to increase your intensity to complete your final set of bench presses at the gym. Here are some strategies for throttling up.

- Take three to five forceful breaths.

- Create a powerful image such as a battleship, a fierce animal, or a volcanic eruption. Or simply picture a successful lift before actually attempting one.

- Make powerful movements such as pumping your fist or clapping your hands.

- Repeat energizing thoughts such as "Yes, I can!" or "Get my A-game on!"

- Recall your favorite up-tempo song.

Throttle down. Perhaps you need to decrease your intensity level between periods of a hockey game or innings of a baseball or softball game. Here are a few ways you can throttle down.

- Take three to five calming breaths.

- Imagine a serene scene such as a cool mountain lake.

- Perform light stretches.

- Think calming thoughts such as "Clear mind, relaxed body."

- Recall your favorite relaxing song.

Most athletes are underactivated for practice ("This doesn't matter") and overactivated for games ("This means everything!"). The next time you are practicing or competing, ask yourself, "Is my intensity level too low, too high, or just right?" Adjust accordingly to achieve your ideal zone for peak performance.

PERSONAL AFFIRMATION WORKS: POWER PHRASES FOR BECOMING A CHAMPION

It's the repetition of affirmations that leads to belief. And once that belief becomes a deep conviction, things begin to happen.

—MUHAMMAD ALI

Attitude is the key source for peak performance. Develop a list of power phrases or positive affirmations to ignite your inner champion. Make sure each statement is meaningful so it really speaks to you. Then write your statements down on index cards and read them for a mental boost as needed. The more often you repeat your power phrases with meaning and conviction, the more concrete they will become in your mind and allow you to manifest change in your life.

"As a single footstep will not make a path on the earth, so a single thought will not make a pathway in the mind. To make a deep physical path, we walk again and again. To make a deep mental path, we must think over and over the kind of thoughts we wish to dominate our lives," wrote author and philosopher Henry David Thoreau.

Anthony Robles of Arizona State University won the 2010–11 NCAA Division I individual wrestling championship in the 125-pound class. Despite being born with only one leg, he rejected any notion of being held back from realizing his athletic dreams. He received the Jimmy V Award for Perseverance at the 2011 ESPY Awards. During his acceptance speech, Robles recited a poem he wrote called "Unstoppable." The poem ends with powerful self-affirmation about fearlessness and perserverance.

Keep to the present tense in creating personal affirmations. For instance, say, "I am" rather than using the future tense, "I will become." Why? Because we always live and perform in present time, not in the future. The subconscious mind does not recognize the future; it only understands the here and now. Here are some power phrases that you can repeat to help you perform at a champion's level:

- I think, feel, and perform as a champion.
- The next play will be my best play.
- I play with purpose and passion.
- I quickly forget mistakes because all athletes make them.
- I have the courage to face and overcome my fears.
- I am the player who is the best prepared.
- I will go through fire to accomplish my goals.
- I strive to be my best in all conceivable ways.
- I *bring it* every day.
- I start strong and finish stronger.

To perform at a champion's level, you must possess and thus need to cultivate a champion's mind-set. The aim of this chapter was to provide you with an increased understanding of the mental side of your game. You now have at your disposal the mental skills—such as mental imagery, confidence, and focus—for creating a champion's mind-set to achieve consistently higher levels of personal performance. Follow the exercises and recommendations provided to build a rock-solid mental approach to your game. As a result, you will manifest better on- and off-the-field performance.

CHAPTER THREE

BE IN IT
TO WIN IT

I play to win, whether during practice or a real game. And I will not let anything get in the way of me and my competitive enthusiasm to win.

—MICHAEL JORDAN

Some athletes play to win the game, others play so as not to lose the game. Some athletes play to make plays, while others play so as not to make mistakes. To perform at a champion's level, you should always play to win by trying to make something positive happen. Besides, it is more enjoyable to go after something of value than to be constantly running for cover.

Always play to win the shot, game, starting position, scholarship, sponsorship, or your personal best times or scores. If you play to not lose, you are placing yourself in a no-win situation; there is everything to lose and nothing to be gained. If you play to win, you are placing yourself in a no-lose situation; by not overcoming the challenge at hand, all you can say is that you did not achieve today's goal. Here are some of the differences between playing to not lose and playing to win:

• Playing so as not to lose is rooted in fear. Playing to win is based in confidence.

- Playing so as not to lose puts you constantly back on your heels. Playing to win keeps you on your toes.

- Playing so as not to lose stymies all of your abilities as you over- or undertry. Playing to win allows you to play within yourself.

- Playing so as not to lose causes muscle tension (and mistakes). Playing to win frees you to perform at your best (tension-free).

- Playing so as not to lose is about merely surviving. Playing to win is about thriving.

- Playing so as not to lose makes for stressful moments. Playing to win creates special moments.

Fear of winning and fear of failing. American soccer star Abby Wambach is a two-time Olympic gold medalist. She says, "You cannot win at everything you attempt in life. You have to be willing to fail and fall flat on your face in order to get glory." This willingness requires that you worry less about what other people might think if you fail and that you take smart risks and play your own game.

As you progress along your sports career path, you will find two fierce opponents against which battles must be fought. These opponents are the fear of winning and the fear of failing; defeat both to achieve your highest aspirations. Which of these inner opponents menaces your game the most? In order to win the battle within, learn to face your fears by taking them head-on. Dare to be your gold self.

Give yourself permission to win unapologetically. Some athletes fear winning big against an opponent or winning a major competition. They may feel that they are not worthy of the reward or they may perhaps shun the spotlight. But consider this: Why not you and why not now? As a talented athlete, you need to develop a sense of deservedness. If you worked hard and intelligently for a positive outcome, then you have already earned the reward, so you should feel proud of your accomplishment. Do not limit yourself to small goals and do not underestimate your personal ability to become more successful. Go for the glory!

Give yourself permission to fall forward. Some athletes fear failing in the big competitions. They might fear that others will think less of them if this happens, or they just don't want to let themselves down. As a capable athlete, all you can do is train correctly and bring your best game to competition. What others may think of you is only their opinion and does not have to be your concern. Don't be too discouraged after delivering an unsuccessful performance. Transform losses into new beginnings or growing pains rather than thinking of them as end points. After all, there is no shortage of competitions and opportunities if you look for them. "Our greatest glory is not in never falling, but in rising each time we fall," stated ancient Chinese philosopher Confucius.

Dan O'Brien used failure to vault himself to greater heights. He was the heavy favorite to claim gold at the 1992 Olympics in Barcelona, but he failed to qualify during the U.S. Olympic trials after scoring zero points in the pole vault. He used this experience as a stepping-stone rather than as a stumbling block. He would go on to break the world record for decathlon points and then capture Olympic gold in 1996 in Atlanta. He says, "Take pride in exactly what it is you do and remember it's okay to fail as long as you don't give up."

Keep pushing in the direction of your goals. Step up, take a risk, and draw on the power of going for gold.

TEAM MOTTOES:
GOLD MEDAL TEAM SLOGANS

Individually, we are one drop. Together, we are an ocean.
—RYŪNOSUKE SATORO, JAPANESE POET

Attitude is the key source for peak team performance. Develop a team slogan or theme for the year to keep everyone inspired and on the same wavelength. Have fun being creative during this brainstorming process. Then, post the slogan where it can be seen as a positive reminder regarding the team mission.

For example, during his successful tenure with the New York Giants, coach Bill Parcells posted a sign in the locker room reflecting his no-nonsense approach: "Blame nobody, expect nothing, do something."

The U.S. Navy SEALs helped inspire the Arizona Diamondbacks to a worst-to-first turnaround in their division for the 2011 baseball season. During spring training, the team received a visit from a trio of SEALs who provided an hour-long talk about their philosophy of mental toughness.

Specifically, the initials DWI were written on a whiteboard and the team was told that when things get difficult, "Deal with It." This straightforward message, which the SEALs live by, became the Diamondbacks team slogan. This is a stance that you can adopt. Deal with whatever you are facing—because you can.

Here are some additional slogans used by athletic teams I have worked with:

- Don't believe the hype—create it!

- Get out of yourself and into the team.

- Teamwork makes the dream work.

- PTAFW: Prove Them All F****** Wrong.

- Delivering on the promise of excellence.

- Out of unity is strength.

- Dare to be great.

- Whatever it takes.

- Think big, play bigger.

- Take PRIDE: Personal Responsibility in Delivering Excellence.

LEAVE EVERYTHING ELSE IN YOUR "MENTAL LOCKER"

Throughout the duration of your practice or game, do not mentally process any personal concerns (e.g., a student-athlete worried about upcoming midterm exams). Leave these burdens in your mental locker when you hit the field, go to the rink, or step on the court.

There's a martial arts expression for when you arrive at the dojo: "Leave the outside, outside." Why? This is because an athlete *distracted* will soon be an athlete *defeated*. Free yourself to switch on (sports mode) so that you funnel all of your energy to the purpose at hand.

If what's troubling you is legitimate, you'll be able to manage it more effectively afterward. Deal with it later in the day, when you aren't in game mode, by setting aside a dedicated time for resolving the issue. There will be an opportunity to turn your undivided attention to it later.

After performing, switch off (nonsports mode) so that you do not end up taking your practice or game home. This will allow you to attend to the other areas of your life, as well as to rest and relax, and to return the next day refreshed and energized. Emphasize the here and now in all realms of your life.

DROP THE GAME FACE

Peak performance is associated with a mental state of relaxed alertness. The intense expression of determination that the game face invokes is merely unwanted muscle tension. Act in accordance with this Chinese proverb: "Tension is who you think you should be. Relaxation is who you are."

Don't be somebody you're not. Stick to how you respond naturally when you are at your best. There is no use trying to artificially ratchet up the intensity by squinting your eyes and making an intense face. Bring your *own* face to the game and play within yourself.

WAIT FOR THE MOMENT OF ACTION

Do you want to win so badly that you become impatient? Hall of Fame NHL goaltender Ed Belfour, who played from 1988 to 2007, said, "You want to win so badly and you want to help the team so badly that you end up trying too much instead of letting the play come to you."

So learn how to wait for your moment in whatever you're playing. Be disciplined, stay patient, and then act decisively. Other examples include: baseball and softball players waiting for *the* pitch, Brazilian jujitsu practitioners waiting to pin their opponent, and running backs in American football waiting to see daylight through the defensive line.

In the moment of action, do you press or force the issue? Do nothing—yet. Stay in "go" mode and then freewheel. Permit your natural, unrestrained talent to flow. Let the play come to you. Bottom line: flow, don't force.

PROCESS, PROCESS, PROCESS

During competition, emphasize what you need to do to win, as opposed to the outcome of winning. That is, focus on the game itself and what you need to do to play well right at this moment.

Enjoy the process of competing in the moment to avoid the temptation to leap into the future. Don't worry about the final outcome until it's time to do so. Thinking only about playing the game, not about the end of the game or outside factors, is the process.

Immerse yourself fully, with your whole being, in what is relevant to your play, keeping away the distractions of the last time, the next time, or the potential result. "What actions do I need to focus on to be successful?" or "What is my immediate target?" are the questions you should be asking, rather than "Are we going to win?" or "Will coach pull me out of the game?" Regardless of the situation, a pitcher should focus all of his or her energy on following a prepitch routine and on hitting the intended spot, pitch by pitch and inning by inning, rather than on needlessly worrying about the scoreboard or anticipating victory.

During practice and preparation, make sure to keep the focus on the process of improvement. A competitive tennis player recently shared with me: "I've noticed that it's quite tough to keep at bay the comments of others who want you to focus on outcome. I've been slowly adding more speed and variety to my tennis footwork, but with each little gain, others see some improvement and actually start having forced expectations. I'm sticking to the plan and process!" To perform at a champion's level, be process oriented in your approach to both practice and competition.

SIMPLICITY IS SUPREME

Athletes tend to complicate their play, as if sports weren't already complicated enough! However, athletes play their best when they have only one dominant thought or image in mind, such as "See ball, hit ball." If you tend to overanalyze or overload your mind, stay target oriented and remind yourself to keep everything as basic as possible. Remember to follow this variation on the KISS principle—Keep It Simple and Straightforward.

Narrow down your thought process so everything is incredibly simple. Here's how sprinter and long jumper Carl Lewis, nine-time Olympic gold medalist and the International Association of Athletics Federations world male athlete of the 20th century, described his own thought process: "My thoughts before a big race are usually pretty simple—get out of the blocks, run your race, stay relaxed."

The champion golfer, for instance, sensibly plots his or her way around the golf course, shot by shot and hole by hole. Such a golfer is on a mission to hit the ball in the fairway, place the ball on the green, and then drain the putt. At most, only one or two swing keys or reminders are employed during the round because the golfer is playing golf, not golf-swing. Or, to put it another way, she is "living in the target" and trying to get the ball in the hole rather than making things unnecessarily technical.

PACE, DON'T RACE

When things go wrong or you feel the pressure increase, everything usually speeds up—your walking pace, rate of speech, and so on. If your inclination is to rush, remind yourself to *slow it down* in order to avoid making errors.

Watch out for the impulse toward racing through a high-pressure situation simply to get it over with. It may be helpful to ride the impulse without giving in or resorting to it.

Breathing deeply and evenly will slow everything down, including your perception of time. Be a Steady Eddie or a Steady Betty while performing by maintaining a consistent mental and physical cadence.

Basketball coaching legend John Wooden had many famous quotes as part of his Pyramid of Success. One of my favorite Woodenisms is "Be quick, but don't hurry." For example, a point guard in basketball or a quarterback in football should play quick and fast while staying cool, calm, and collected.

CELEBRATE WHAT YOU WANT TO SEE HAPPEN MORE OFTEN

Periodically review your performance high points, personal bests, and magic moments. Revisit the celebratory feelings you had and pay attention to that sense of greatness. Then bring those experiences to bear on future situations. Take time to pause and reflect on what was good and what worked. These highlights offer a hint of your total potential.

Too often, like a Monday-morning quarterback armed with hindsight, we think back to what went wrong or what we did not do rather than what went well or what we accomplished. All of our positive plays and personal victories are hard-earned prizes. Reward yourself for a job well done by keeping success fresh in your mind.

Always plan to celebrate what you have done well and learn from feedback so that you can do even better the next time. For positive reinforcement, give yourself a mental fist bump when you make a good quality play or go two for two in a competition by bringing a positive attitude and your full effort from start to finish. Do not overestimate your defeats. Do not undervalue your successes, either.

LAUNCH A COMEBACK
WHEN YOU NEED ONE

When you do not achieve a peak performance in the first half of a game, you can always bring your performance back up again in the second half. A champion takes pride in being a comeback specialist.

Instead of dwelling on the negative ("I haven't done anything good all day"), become a resilient performer by thinking that something good is always just about to happen. Stay positive to keep momentum on your side.

During the 1927 Wimbledon semifinal, Henri Cochet of France was on the brink of elimination in his match against American Bill Tilden, the two-time men's singles Wimbledon champion. Cochet had dropped the first two sets and was down 1–5 in the third set. However, Cochet refused to lose; incredibly, he rallied to a five-set victory and earned a spot in the Wimbledon finals.

"I've always made a total effort, even when the odds seemed entirely against me. I never quit trying; I never felt that I didn't have a chance," stated Arnold Palmer, one of the greatest players in the history of golf. Palmer was in 15th place and trailing by seven strokes heading into the final round of the 1960 U.S. Open at Cherry Hills Country Club near Denver, Colorado. Down but not done, Palmer started his day with four birdies in a row on his way to an epic come-from-behind win.

In the 1992 AFC wild card playoff game, the Buffalo Bills were getting drilled on their home field by the Houston Oilers. The Bills were losing 35–3 in the third quarter. However, the Bills didn't roll over, stampeding from behind to go on and win in overtime.

American gymnast Jordyn Wieber, the 2011 world all-around

champion, failed to make the all-around finals in the qualifying round at the 2012 London Olympics despite being the clear favorite. Although Wieber had one of the best scores of the day, she took third to teammates Gabby Douglas and Aly Raisman, and only two gymnasts per country are allowed to compete in the all-around. Wieber burst into tears upon learning that she had been eliminated. Her dreams of winning all-around gold had turned into a nightmare after a lifetime of focus and effort.

A true champion (and teammate), Wieber was able to grieve the loss, turn the page, and confidently move forward with the help and full support of her family and team. She was back competing just 48 hours after the most disappointing performance of her stellar career. Putting "we" over "me," she came out focused, nailed the vault event, and helped the United States capture team gold for the first time since 1996.

A minor setback provides an opportunity for making a major comeback. As Yogi Berra famously said, "It ain't over 'til it's over." Always run *through* the finish line regardless of how far you are behind (or ahead) during competition. After a bad start to a season, stay affirmative to finish on a high note. Resolve never to give up or let up in your own game.

LOVE THE GRIND

There is always a way to get the job done—even when you are struggling in one area of your game. When you are not at the top of your game and are thus unable to reproduce your best form, just figure out how to close the deal on that day.

When you are struggling with your driver in golf, win with your short game. When your shots aren't dropping in basketball, be a glove on defense. Step up your game rather than throw in the towel. Refuse to quit even when a scenario seems bleak or hopeless.

Take a minute right now to think about your performances when you did not believe a good or respectable outcome was possible but you still found a way to make it happen. There is beauty in being ugly but effective (UBE) or having a good bad day (GBD) while you are not at your finest. Keep your head in the game and grind it out.

Rory McIlroy, a four-time major champion, won the 2011 Shanghai Masters on the first hole of a playoff, despite giving up an early three-shot lead and having to rally from a stroke down on the back nine to force the playoff against Anthony Kim. This is how McIlroy described his mind-set after winning in Shanghai without his A-game during the final round:

> Something that I feel like I can still get better at is winning and putting yourself in the position to win when you're not playing your best. Even if it's scrappy golf where you grind it out, you're going to win a lot more tournaments by doing that rather than playing your best golf the whole week. I was very happy I was able to pull this one out.

STAY IN ATHLETE MODE

Do you ever describe the sports action to yourself as if you were your own on-field reporter? Athletes in self-paced sports such as golf, target shooting, and tennis tend to have a running inner dialogue about how well they are performing. They may overanalyze their technique, continuously compare themselves to others, and constantly project their final score. Such inner commentary keeps you one step removed from the actual performance, rather than fully focused on the performance.

Always be athletic on the field of play. Do not take on the additional role of being your own coach, parent, spectator, or shrink. Stay in athlete mode by focusing all of your energy on execution, not self-analysis. Don't write the review of your performance until after it is over. Let the final score take care of itself while you take care of yourself. If you often worry about what spectators are thinking, pretty soon you will join them on the sidelines!

DO WHAT YOU HAVE BEEN COACHED TO DO

Your job when you play is not to win or please others—that's beyond your control. Instead, your job is to do what you have been coached to do by carrying out your specific assignments with the right attitude to the best of your abilities—that's within your control. Doing your job or what you are supposed to do puts you in the best position for you and your team to succeed. If you do the right things, such as following coaching instructions, you are more likely to have a winning outcome.

New England Patriots head coach Bill Belichick has six Super Bowl rings, four as a head coach. He constantly reminds his players: "Know what your job is and do your job." Knowing your responsibilities and doing your job is how you can magnify the relevant aspects of your performance while shrinking everything that is irrelevant. Embracing your role on the team is how you can be true to what it is you are doing. This will help your own cause and make it easier for your teammates to do their jobs.

GET "MAD DECISIVE"

Anxiety shapes you up and sharpens your focus—but only a moderate amount of anxiety. Anger is our instinctive defense against feeling scared; however, a *little* anger can provide pleasure, power, motivation, and relief from anxiety.

As such, if you are overanxious prior to a game or unmotivated before practice, think of something that makes you a little mad, such as a real or perceived slight—the opponent who talked trash or maybe the last time your team lost. Positively funneling this "game-on" feeling into your performance is often more effective than trying to relax or calm down when overanxious.

Swimmer Michael Phelps is the only athlete to win eight gold medals in a single Olympics, a feat he accomplished in Beijing in 2008. He confessed to using doubts about him that were publicly expressed by his competitors as fire in his stomach for training. Phelps revealed, "If people want to talk, I encourage it, because I love it. It motivates me more than anything." What fires *you* with motivation?

Boxer Lennox Lewis won gold for Canada at the 1988 Seoul Olympics and has the distinction of being the last undisputed world heavyweight champion. He explained the importance of being driven by competitiveness rather than rage: "Rage takes energy, and I want to keep my energy focused. If a man hits me, I'll think, 'Good for you, that's a good shot.'"

It is always better to refrain from raging or getting "mad destructive"; swearing, fighting, or throwing things is self-defeating and evidence of poor sportsmanship. There are better channels for expressing your dissatisfaction. Have a positive physical way of releasing frustration after making a poor play, such as by clapping your hands. Being "mad decisive" is how you stay classy by appropriately and professionally channeling your competitive drive.

ASK YOURSELF
THE RIGHT QUESTIONS

Recall that thoughts determine feelings, and then feelings influence performance. This being true, ask yourself questions that lead to positive thoughts and problem solving, especially when you are worried or distressed. Focus on the situation—at that moment—decide, and act.

Good questions include "What do I want to happen?" or "What would help me now?" Keep focused for good results. Bad questions such as "Why is this happening now?" or "What's wrong with me?" lack satisfactory answers and thus bring bad consequences. Ask, "What is my inner champion telling me to do *here* and *now*? Or, "What would [a person you admire] do *here* and *now*?" The second question puts the person you admire in your situation, even if that person did not play your sport. Thinking about the person you admire will provide you with his or her motivation and strength.

On game day, the key question is "What do I need to do to perform my best?" The mental challenge is to stay in your "own zone" by focusing on your performance and what you want to accomplish. Listen to breaststroke swimmer Amanda Beard, a seven-time Olympic medalist (including two gold medals): "I concentrate on preparing to swim my race and let the other swimmers think about me, not me about them."

PUT SOME MUSIC ON YOUR MIND

Are you "in tune" or "on beat" while you are exercising or playing? Listening to great music is one of the best and quickest ways to improve your mood, stay in the moment, and find your intensity and game-time rhythm.

- Professional snowboarder and skateboarder Shaun White, a two-time Olympic gold medalist, says, "Music gets me in the rhythm I want before the run."

- Mariano Rivera, former ace relief pitcher for the New York Yankees, would enter to Metallica's "Enter Sandman" when he would come in from the bullpen in Yankee Stadium.

- Former NFL Baltimore Ravens superstar linebacker Ray Lewis says that he would get pumped up to the inspirational song "In the Air Tonight" by Phil Collins before every game.

So what motivating song(s) do you listen to before games? Develop a personalized playlist for generating emotions that match your activities, such as getting ready for practicing or competing or winding down at night.

Make (or update) your personal pump-up playlist for training. Include your favorite mix of up-tempo songs that get you psyched right to go the distance.

Here are a few power-song suggestions to help you maximize your workout:

1. "Enter Sandman"—Metallica

2. "Pump It"—Black Eyed Peas

3. "Go Getta"—Young Jeezy

4. "Lose Yourself"—Eminem

5. "Intro"—The xx

6. "Thunderstruck"—AC/DC

7. "Drown in the Now"—The Crystal Method (featuring Matisyahu)

8. "Remember the Name"—Fort Minor

9. "Welcome to the Jungle"—Guns N' Roses

10. "Through the Fire"—Pete Miser

11. "Can't Hold Us"—Macklemore and Ryan Lewis

12. "Seven Nation Army"—The White Stripes

PSYCH IN, NOT OUT

Hyperbole fogs up the challenge at hand. It doesn't help to be melodramatic about the state of affairs and think pressure views like "The stakes are high," "The other team is unbeatable," "This shot is impossible," or "This is do or die!" Mental clarity is just that—clear—and a balanced perspective isn't foggy.

Realize that all these self-psych-outs, even if said in jest, will pile on the pressure and increase muscle tension, diminishing the likelihood that you will perform at your peak. Play your game with inspiration, not desperation.

Regardless of your competition or your circumstances, ask yourself only to do your best, as that is all you can do. In sports and in life, difficulty is a constant, but exaggeration is constantly changing, so it is always best to keep things "real" in the moment.

MAKE PLAYS, NOT EXCUSES

A champion adheres to the "no-excuse rule." Some athletes come up with prepractice cop-outs to take the easy way out or make precompetition excuses in the event they don't perform well; however, the excuse they find can set up a self-fulfilling prophecy that actually generates the poor results they had hoped to avoid.

It is always better to go with what you've got; no excuses (psychological crutches) are needed. Even when you are not feeling your best or circumstances aren't ideal, you can still succeed. Just tell yourself, "I can still play well and concentrate on what I need to do."

Postcompetition excuses, such as blaming others, are designed to deflect personal responsibility and save face following an unwanted outcome. Instead, think, "I did not play my best, and I will work hard to make the necessary positive corrections." In other words, take full responsibility for your play—both wins and losses.

McKayla Maroney was a member of the gold-medal-winning U.S. women's gymnastics team at the 2012 Summer Olympics. Maroney, the reigning world vault champion, was expected to win Olympic gold in her individual event, and led after the first attempt. However, she slid to second place in the standings after she lost her footing during the landing on her second try. She remarked, "I didn't deserve to win gold if I landed on my butt." Although in this statement she comes across as being really hard on herself, Maroney took full responsibility for the finish instead of making excuses.

Maintain a champion attitude to avoid making these three common excuses:

• Excuse 1: "The ref screwed us!"
  Champion attitude: "We need to learn how to beat the other team and any bad calls that are made."

• Excuse 2: "My team/coach sucks!"
  Champion attitude: "I fully support, and cheer on, all of my teammates and coaches."

• Excuse 3: "The other team got lucky!"
  Champion attitude: "Maybe the other team was lucky; now let's turn on our luck," or "The other team had better stuff today; let's figure out a way to beat them next time."

IMPROVISE, ADAPT, AND OVERCOME

The best-laid plans never go without a hitch. To perform at a champion's level, imagine what-ifs well in advance and always draw up effective contingency plans through problem-solving phrases such as "If x happens, I'll do y." That way, when bad or unexpected things do occur, you won't be shocked or unnerved; you will possess the mental tools and flexibility to deal with unplanned events.

Having a champion's mind-set—by avoiding blame, staying focused on a solution, and showing a good sense of humor—will alleviate your fear because you'll know you can handle any hardship or inconvenience that comes your way. Most of the time, when the unexpected happens, all you'll need to do is make minor adjustments and ignore whatever isn't essential to performing your best. Focus on your intended target, and potential distractions will recede into the background.

Delays and interruptions will at most be hassles, not horror stories. As examples, consider dealing with slow play on the golf course, arriving late to a competition, or handling a long rain delay. These situations are unfortunate but not the end of the world. They call forth a mantra that is repeated in many U.S. military units: "Improvise, adapt, and overcome."

Improvise, adapt, and overcome any and all disruptions rather than permitting them to ruin your day or your performance. Remain positive and patient. Positive self-talk can take the shape of phrases such as "I can handle this even though I may not like it." Take a breath, compose yourself, and move confidently forward. You can also hum a tune or sing a song to maintain your rhythm if that helps.

To perform at a champion's level, always problem-solve ways to cope rather than mope when the unexpected happens. This mental flexibility is as important at the Olympics as it is at any other competition. During the 2008 Beijing Olympics, Misty May-Treanor and Kerri Walsh Jennings battled through several unpredictable events in their successful quest for winning back-to-back beach volleyball gold medals. However, they always stayed fiercely positive no matter what happened on the court.

In her moving memoir, *Misty: My Journey Through Volleyball and Life*, May-Treanor describes the unforeseen challenges: They did not receive their tailored swimsuits on time and had to wear another brand; May-Treanor came down with a cold and fever; Walsh Jennings lost her wedding ring during their match against Japan; they had to compete against a just-formed Brazilian partnership; and, finally, they had to play for the gold medal in driving rain against China's top duo, a team that had an overwhelming home-court advantage.

THAT'S ME

What do you tell yourself immediately after you've made a good play or delivered a solid performance? Your affirmative self-talk needs to include "That's me. I will keep doing what I'm doing, and I will keep playing the way I'm playing."

For example, a quarterback completes his Second Pass of the game right on target to his receiver. This confident quarterback thinks, "I've already completed two out of two attempts because I will complete my next pass."

Think of success as long-lasting and believe you are destined for good things. Now, what do you tell yourself immediately after you've had a not-so-good play or performance? Affirmative (never negative) self-talk needs to include "That's not like me. That was just a blip. Now I'll adjust and turn this around."

For example, a quarterback misfires on his Second Pass by over-throwing his receiver. The still-confident quarterback thinks, "I've already completed one out of two attempts because my next pass will be right on target."

Think of failure as short-lived—soon replaced by success. Always believe that a disappointment is replaced by your next success.

YOU CAN'T DO
A "DON'T DO"

Focus on what you want to happen, not what you are afraid might happen. A classic example is the novice golfer who thinks, "I better not hit the ball in the water" and then proceeds to do exactly that.

How can you hit the clutch shots? Just look and do or aim and fire. Michael Jordan burst onto the basketball scene when he hit the game-winning shot as the University of North Carolina defeated Georgetown to win the 1982 NCAA basketball championship. He said, "I never looked at the consequences of missing a big shot; when you think about the consequences, you always think of a negative result."

Rather than trying to perform *without* fear, strive to perform *with* confidence. Affirmative self-talk needs to take the shape of phrases like "I can do this!" rather than "Don't blow it"; "Stay on target!" instead of "Block out distractions"; or "Hang tough!" in lieu of "Don't quit now."

PRESSURE IS A PRIVILEGE, NOT A PROBLEM

Pressure is always in the mind of the beholder. In other words, an athlete's feelings and behaviors on game day are driven by immediate situations and the athlete's interpretation of them. Some athletes, like tennis champion Billie Jean King, view pressure as a privilege, while others deem pressure as a sign that something has gone awry.

Athletes will experience intense pressure in their performance as long as they perceive athletic contests as an impending disaster rather than a great opportunity. Furthermore, these athletes also have a tendency to interpret normal bodily sensations, such as an increased heart rate prior to performing, as catastrophic. Importantly, this type of "bad" pressure can be clobbered by developing the right mind-set.

For example, consider Seattle Seahawks quarterback Russell Wilson. Discussing his mind-set while under pressure, Wilson said, "I love it when the game is on the line, when everyone else is nervous and I'm excited." Along the same lines, UFC veteran fighter Vitor Belfort explained, "I just do my best so there is no pressure." When you are feeling tense and uptight from pressure, try reframing the situation. This is a technique for helping people see their situation in a better light, from a winning perspective.

The mental challenge is to change from a negative to a positive point of view. Instead of being in a high-pressure situation, think of this moment as your occasion to thrive. Welcome the challenge at hand because there really is nothing to lose and so much to gain. You will either win or learn from your performance. Understanding this perspective will help you maintain a "be in it to win it" mind-set rather than playing to simply not lose.

The perception of "bad" pressure or danger leads to a complex chain of biochemical events resulting in overstimulation—a pounding heart, sweaty palms, and a whirling mind. As such, it is very important to practice performing with this increased stimulation and learn to work with it.

All coaches and athletes understand the importance of making a portion of practice time pressurized, realistic, and more competitive to help mentally prepare for competition. However, simply imagining that you are in the actual situation, playing loud music to simulate crowd noise, or making small bets can be useful but incomplete approaches.

Directly simulating the stress response is a key concept. Elevate your heart rate and get your arms shaky by doing pushups, running in place, or doing jumping jacks for 60 to 90 seconds or so. Take a few really deep breaths. Now rehearse your free throw shot, golf swing, field goal kick, or tennis serve the best that you can in spite of the nerves.

Simulating the stress response in this manner while in the practice environment will provide greater assurance over time that you can manage your emotional and physical states and perform on command, especially when your adrenaline is spiking in a championship situation.

TRUST YOUR TALENT

Avoid the perils of perfectionism and survive the "paralysis-by-analysis" syndrome—underperforming by overthinking. Let your body do what you've trained it to do.

Go external with your focus rather than being internally preoccupied with technique or the mechanical aspects. Get out of your head and get into your performance. Trust that all your skills are right at your fingertips.

Accept that you are prepared, free yourself to perform, and let it fly. This attitude will help you be more artistic and fluid in your performance, and this is imperative at key moments or in close games.

"Train it and trust it," advises famed sports psychologist Bob Rotella. Here are the three steps of the train-it-and-trust-it process.

1. The first step is to train your talent in practice.

2. The second step is to trust your talent in competition.

3. The third step is to keep *repeating* the first two steps.

All champions and top teams understand that trust is a must for peak performance. Curt Tomasevicz is a two-time Olympian and member of the Night Train four-man bobsled team, along with Steven Holcomb, Justin Olsen, and Steve Langton (who replaced Steve Mesler). Team Night Train won the first gold medal for the United States in 62 years in four-man bobsledding at the Vancouver Winter Olympics in 2010. Tomasevicz shared with me his thoughts on the importance of trust. He explained:

> One of my favorite Olympic moments occurred just before the final run. As my team was preparing for the last of the four runs at the 2010 Olympics, I remember taking a brief moment to really "trust my talent." We had a significant lead after the first day (two runs) and an even bigger lead after the first run on the second day. (The winner is determined by the fastest sum of the four runs). So going into the last run, just as we finished our warmup and walked to the start line, there could have been the thought of "Don't blow the huge lead," which would have created unnecessary pressure and tension. Or we could have played the last run cautiously and conservatively and have been too lackadaisical. Instead we

simply looked at each other confidently and approached the final run as we had the previous thousand runs of our careers. We knew that we simply had to do what we did that got us to that point: trust our ability and not be overly excited or cautious. We did nothing different than we did in the first three runs of the race and just let the cream rise to the top.

Always be in it to win it. As we've discussed, some athletes play to win the game, whereas others play to not lose the game. Don't limit your mind and body with restrictions; free yourself to perform. Your mind-set is that you have nothing to lose and everything to gain. Always try to make something positive happen in your game and life by incorporating the mental strategies offered in this chapter.

Knowing the importance of going for the gold in your game, are you focusing on the process rather than the outcome? Are you going to celebrate more often what you want to see happen? Are you going to emulate gold medalist Curt Tomasevicz by letting your best rise to the top in the moment of action? Free up your mind to win. You're going for gold!

CHAPTER FOUR

THE WISDOM OF A CHAMPION

I learned that if you want to make it bad enough,
no matter how bad it is, you can make it.

—GALE SAYERS

S o far we have been building mental muscle with the key mental skills and strategies needed to perform in your sport with a champion's mind-set. You've learned how to think, feel, and play like a champion because the mentality of an athlete is the main variable in terms of who gets the "W" or who achieves personal best times and scores. This chapter offers further strategies that provide psychological insights to help rocket your game to newer dimensions and higher levels. You will begin to see your sports performance from an exceptional and more commanding viewpoint.

TAKE A MASTERY APPROACH

There are two types of athletes: those who seek awards, admiration, and other such accolades above all else, and those who truly love their sport and are driven to find out how well they can play. The former are classified as having an *ego orientation;* they are thrilled when they receive recognition and are devastated when they do not. The latter are defined as having a *mastery approach;* they generally appreciate everything about the process of striving for personal excellence, regardless of the end result.

For instance, ego-oriented student-athletes may be excessively concerned with their stats on the field (e.g., batting average) and GPAs in the classroom. This orientation is associated with higher levels of performance anxiety, as well as discouragement in the face of failures or setbacks, because motivation is mostly contingent on extrinsic factors, such as others' opinions. Furthermore, there can be an overwhelming sense of emptiness for ego-oriented athletes after accomplishing their top goal because they are looking in the wrong place to find personal happiness. They can only wonder, "What next?" without ever discovering a satisfactory answer to their question.

In contrast, student-athletes who approach tasks with an orientation toward mastery are mainly motivated by intrinsic rewards, such as love of the game and pursuit of growth and development. They continually seek to improve on the field and gain wisdom in the classroom. They have fun taking part in practices and games, as well as participating in class discussions. Rewards that are external to the process of participation and competition are purely icing on the cake. Their outlook is more about thoroughly enjoying the journey rather than simply reaching a particular destination.

My professional observation has been that the happiest and most accomplished athletes are those who take a mastery approach, regardless of their particular specialization. Such people are driven by curiosity and enjoyment as much as outer success. Paradoxically, athletes who appreciate the process rather than obsess about outcome often find that they attract better outcomes. Seattle Seahawks quarterback Russell Wilson is a prime example of someone with a mastery approach. He says, "I have this rage to master my craft." Wilson channels his competitive nature and passion for football into his daily pursuits, whether studying film or practicing his footwork, in order to excel on game day.

To achieve personal and competitive greatness, search for motivation wherever you can find it. Enjoy the spoils of victory, such as the applause of the crowd or the trophy for winning a championship. However, true motivation always comes from within. Make participating in and enjoying the activity itself your biggest reward. In competition, rather than worrying about what will get recorded on the score sheet, emphasize your mental game stats, such as attitude and hustle. Doing so will keep your motivation at a higher level and lead to more in-the-zone experiences. Always compete. Always battle. Never settle in the quest for your personal best, and outer success will soon follow you.

BE YOUR OWN TOUGHEST RIVAL

A central concept for becoming a champion is to battle against your best or gold self. Do not accept a silver or bronze attitude and effort level. Pro Football Hall of Fame quarterback Steve Young said, "The principle is competing against yourself. It's about self-improvement, about being better than you were the day before." In other words, always try to win against your own standard of excellence and keep raising the bar on your own level of play.

LeBron James shared with reporters during the 2012–13 NBA season that he was waging a "vendetta" against himself in an effort to take his game up another notch. His declaration about trying to progress as a player came *after* being named 2012 Sports Illustrated Sportsman of the Year for winning an NBA championship and an Olympic gold medal, and being named both league MVP and finals MVP.

Additionally, use great performances by others as extra inspiration for your own improvement. Challenge your teammates or other top competitors in order to push yourself to higher and higher levels. Compete against your teammates in practice, but then support them during games. It is always better to develop productive rivalries with all your teammates and competitors rather than to harbor negative jealousies.

Tomasz Majewski of Poland won shot put gold at the 2012 London Olympics, becoming the first man since Parry O'Brien in 1952 and 1956 to win back-to-back titles. Majewski was considered somewhat of an underdog in both the 2008 and 2012 games. Earlier in his career he had remarked, "The good performances of my rivals [don't] make me angry or worried; instead they act as the best sort of motivation to get up to their level."

SHINE WHILE YOU CAN

"To be what we are, and to become what we are capable of becoming, is the only end of life," wrote Robert Louis Stevenson, one of the most famous writers of the 19th century. Our opportunity to shine in the game of life and in athletics is fleeting—the clock is ticking. So go the extra mile, lap, or hill with a fresh sense of purpose and passion. Being a champion means fully expressing yourself and doing all the things you value in your life. Leave your comfort zone behind and deliberately and fiercely chase your dream goals. Run hard down the field and carry the ball over the goal line.

SUCCESS IS PEACE OF MIND

Strive to always bring a winning attitude and steady effort to practice and competition. "Success is peace of mind, which is a direct result of self-satisfaction in knowing you made the effort to do your best to become the best that you are capable of becoming," asserted basketball coaching legend John Wooden. And, Hockey Hall of Famer Gordie Howe, a four-time Stanley Cup champion with the Detroit Red Wings, said, "You find that you have peace of mind and can enjoy yourself, get more sleep, and rest when you know that it was a 100 percent effort that you gave—win or lose."

STAY STRONG IN SELF-BELIEF

Performance success depends on three types of core beliefs: your view of the activity, of yourself, and of the future. Our entrenched self-limiting beliefs are often the biggest barrier to overcome. As such, affirmative self-talk needs to take the shape of phrases such as "I'm up for this challenge," "I'm a champion in the making," and "The sky is the limit if I really put my mind to it." Replace self-defeatist expectations ("I'll never get this skill right") with positive reminders ("I can master this skill with continued practice and patience").

Champions are always willing to learn from constructive criticism. They also believe in themselves regardless of others' negative opinions. Jim Craig, goalie for the American team that won the men's ice hockey gold medal at the 1980 Winter Olympics in Lake Placid, stayed strong in self-belief throughout the games. Here's how Craig explained the importance of self-belief and making a commitment to prove the doubters wrong in his outstanding book *Gold Medal Strategies: Business Lessons from America's Miracle Team*:

> Realize that the world is full of experts who have been
> proven wrong. If you want to find someone to doubt you,
> or locate a cynic, the search won't take long nor be dif-
> ficult. Believe in yourself—even if you are the only one
> who believes in you.

Never let negative comments from others or self-defeating beliefs about your performance go unchallenged. Besides, feeling that you are unworthy or incapable does not mean it is a fact. As golf-swing instructors like to say, what you feel is not always real. What we learned in the past can be transformed by what we learn in the present. Shatter your self-limiting beliefs and also have fun trying to accomplish things that no one else thinks you can. Achieve more by channeling negativity from naysayers into extra effort.

MANAGE YOUR LIMITATIONS

Focus on your strengths and find ways to limit the impact of your limitations. British rower Sir Steve Redgrave won gold medals at five consecutive Olympic Games from 1984 to 2000. After being diagnosed with type 2 diabetes in 1997, he declared, "Diabetes has to live with me, not me live with it." Redgrave made the necessary nutritional corrections to his diet and continued with his relentless pursuit of Olympic excellence. Always strive to limit the impact of your limitations on your ambitions. Remember that a true champion performance means doing the very best you can with whatever abilities you have.

DON'T BE MISTAKEN ABOUT MISTAKES

During competition, *quickly* forget mistakes. This is crucial in largely reactive sports such as boxing or basketball because dwelling on a mistake often leads to making another or even bigger mistake. Keep moving forward by breaking off the rearview mirror. To perform at a champion's level, avoid making it a history lesson while you are in the ring or on the court.

Skiing is another case in point. Alpine ski racer Lindsey Vonn won the gold medal in downhill at the Vancouver Winter Olympics in 2010. She advises, "When you fall, get right back up. Just keep going, keep pushing it." After the race, you can acknowledge and learn from your performance gaffes.

Here is a popular sports psychology technique for symbolically letting go of mistakes in self-paced sports such as baseball and softball: Pick up a blade of grass (or pebble, etc.) after a mistake. Regard the blade of grass as if it were the actual mistake. Now throw the blade of grass (i.e., the mistake) away and refocus on the purpose at hand.

FAILURE CAN BE A GREAT TEACHER

Basketball Hall of Famer Michael Jordan, winner of six NBA titles and two Olympic gold medals, is one of modern history's most accomplished athletes. However, one of the main things Jordan has always emphasized is that the reason he succeeded is because he failed: "I've missed more than 9,000 shots in my career. I've lost almost 300 games. Twenty-six times, I've been trusted to take the game-winning shot and missed. I've failed over and over and over again in my life. And that is why I succeed."

Accept that temporary failures and flubs are an integral part of sports and life. It is also through our failures and continuing to take chances that we eventually succeed. Failure is a wonderful teacher if we learn the lessons it has to teach us and then act on them. Keep working on your game and failure will in time be replaced by success. "The arrow that hits the bull's-eye is the result of 100 misses" is a Buddhist saying that is definitely worth bearing in mind.

SMASH IDOLS

Admire, rather than idolize, your favorite players or you are discounting yourself and your own game. There is no need ever to be in awe of a fellow competitor or any competition. Refuse to be intimidated by anyone or anything. A good adage to follow in your game play is "Don't be intimidated by the impossibility, be motivated by the possibility."

Regardless of others' past accomplishments, nobody is a superhero with special powers; instead, he or she is just another fallible person. Treat everyone with respect, but never treat yourself with disrespect.

Never diminish your own powers by putting yourself down. On the flip side, if you look down on others, make sure it's only because you're helping them stand up or because you're shaking their hands from the top of the medal stand.

In 2000, Tiger Woods had the best year of golf since Ben Hogan's watershed 1953 season. Specifically, Woods won nine tournaments, including three major championships. However, Hal Sutton publicly refused to share the growing defeatist view of his peers. Sutton went on to claim victory over Woods at the 2000 Players Championship.

"Tiger Woods is not bigger than the game," Sutton said after the tournament. "The other night I was lying in bed and I said,

'You know what? I'm not praying to him. He's not a god. He's human just like I am, so we can do this.'"

DON'T BE TOO PROUD TO GET HELP

A champion desires continuous improvement across the board. As such, seek help for needed improvements from specialists with unique skills, such as a sports psychologist, performance trainer, athletic trainer, sports nutritionist, sports medicine doctor, sports chiropractor, or other specially trained individual.

Asking for help or support from a specialist is not an admission of weakness. Rather, it is an acknowledgment that you are human and that you want to hone your performance or enhance your life. For example, a counselor can help us all better understand and solve any underlying personal concerns that might interfere with our performance.

Working with others, particularly experts who can help you achieve your goals, is the antithesis of weakness. Instead, it shows strength of character and resolve to be the best you can be. A Japanese proverb says, "Better than a thousand days of diligent study is one day with a great teacher."

STRENGTH COMES IN THE STRUGGLE

German philosopher Friedrich Nietzsche famously declared, "Whatever doesn't kill me makes me stronger." During a discussion pertaining to this principle, a client of mine joked, "Whatever doesn't kill me just pisses me off."

Adversity is what you make of it. Use unfavorable experiences and events to your advantage, because adversity will come. Rather than viewing adversity as a sign that things are getting worse, be inspired by the opportunity to make your game better. The choice is whether to allow adversity to become a hindrance to your game or to use it to make yourself stronger.

To become stronger and achieve victory over adversity, embrace challenges in life rather than avoiding them or hoping for smooth sailing all of the time. In fact, it is precisely because of obstacles and interferences in our path—and learning how to handle them—that we are able to reach greater degrees of excellence.

Wilma Rudolph is a prime example of victory over adversity. Inspirationally, Rudolph overcame several serious childhood health problems, including a crippled left leg that required the use of metal braces at age 6, to become the fastest woman in the world. She struck gold in the 100 meters, 200 meters, and 4 x 100-meter relay at the 1960 Rome Olympics to become the first American woman to win three events in track and field during a single Olympics. Rudolph said, "The triumph can't be had without the struggle."

CRACKING THE STARTING LINEUP

In his play *Cato, a Tragedy*, English playwright Joseph Addison wrote, "We cannot insure success, but we can deserve it." This philosophy offers insight to how you can handle the disappointment of being in a backup role. Stay patient and persistent when things are not yet the way you want them to be. Channel any frustration in a positive, productive direction. Try your best to become better, whether it is through individual work, team practice, or studying film. Continue to go hard in training and act as if you are in the starting lineup rather than succumbing to defeatist thinking (e.g., "What's the point?"). When you are sitting on the bench, stay upbeat and root for your teammates. Visualize yourself making plays on the court or field while you follow the action. Be mentally ready to go when your name is called.

NOTHING WORKS WITHOUT THE WORK

Align your ambitions, dreams, and goals with reality. Effort and work are needed for improvement and results. If you really want to succeed, then the effort and work are not that tough. Are you practicing to practice or are you working to get better? To perform at a champion's level, understand that "practice is everything," as Seattle Seahawks head coach Pete Carroll says.

Good old-fashioned hard work will pay dividends in future competitions. Rehearse and re-rehearse all of your skills and routines through high-quality training until they are committed to muscle memory and can be performed instinctively on the field of play. Maximum preparation in training leads to optimal performance in competition.

CHASE YOUR WEAKNESSES, BUILD YOUR STRENGTHS

Make sure to work on all parts of your game rather than becoming complacent. Always chase your weaknesses and build your strengths, like all-time great pitcher and batter Lisa Fernandez, three-time Olympic gold medalist with the U.S. softball team. Fernandez explained, "I make my weaknesses my strength, and my strengths stronger." Working on the weaknesses in your game may not always be fun, but it's the fastest path to improvement.

Boston Red Sox second baseman Dustin Pedroia may be small at 5 foot 8, but he posts big numbers on the baseball field. Pedroia's work ethic brings nonstop hustle to everything he does. This is how Pedroia, the 2008 American League MVP, described his off-season training approach in his inspirational book *Born to Play: My Life in the Game*:

> I try to have fun working out, but I look at the off-season as a time to build up enough stamina to last eight months. I watch everything I eat, and I'm working out all the time. In the season, you're maintaining the fitness for eight months. In the off-season, you have three months to make the most gain possible, to become better.

MOVE THE CHAINS

In American football, moving the chains means gaining first downs. Keep making strides or positive yardage to move the chains downfield in the direction of your goals rather than being content at the line of scrimmage. This does not mean that you will score points on every possession or always have a winning outcome. To perform at a champion's level, put steady effort into getting better, covering all aspects of your mind, body, technique, and game strategy.

We can all get mentally and physically stronger and progress as a performer in whatever the sport or fitness activity. You can master the technical skills in your sport and learn how to expertly apply those skills in tactical situations. Improvements and learning experiences, whether minor or major, are meaningful. All progress is a beautiful thing because baby steps and small gains really do add up. Remember the saying "It takes 10 years to become an overnight success."

"What can I do today to move the chains?" This is a crucial question to ask yourself, whether the answer is eating a balanced breakfast, arriving early to the practice field, or just getting a good night's sleep. Always stay positive, patient, and persistent during your progression. Ride out the inevitable slips, setbacks, and plateaus that every performer goes through without letting up or giving in. Recognize that these types of situations are often just normal variations in your performance.

Moving the chains in your sports career is a process, and you will never know when precisely it's all going to fall in place. Some athletes break through early in their careers. One such example is forward Kevin Durant of the NBA's Oklahoma City Thunder. Among his many individual accomplishments, he became at age 21 the youngest player ever to win the NBA scoring title, by averaging 30.1 points per game during the 2009–10 season.

Stay optimistic, because some athletes take longer before reaching superstar status or their best level. Let's take a look at some of the late bloomers in sports:

- Undefeated heavyweight champion Rocky Marciano did not take up boxing until age 20, when he joined the army. He turned pro at age 25.

- Hall of Fame MLB pitcher Sandy Koufax had a rather pedestrian career until age 27.

- Two-time MVP and Super Bowl champion quarterback Kurt Warner made his first NFL start at age 28.

- Chinese professional tennis player Li Na won her first Grand Slam event, the 2011 French Open singles title, at age 29.

- Golf marvel Ben Hogan battled swing problems for years, becoming arguably the best ball-striker ever and winning his first of nine major championships at age 34.

PRIME TIME IS ALL THE TIME

Some athletes tend to sink rather than sail in pressure-filled situations—whether in the first few minutes in round one of college basketball's March Madness, serving for match point, or taking the game-winning shot—because they overplay their game, thinking they need to be better or different than they have been in previous situations.

The mental and physical skills needed, however, remain the same, regardless of a situation's perceived magnitude. Think of practice as the championship and the championship as practice. Nothing extra special is required in a big-game scenario. Stick to your regular pregame routine as much as possible. Get settled right away and keep it happening as you always do.

Trying to prove that your team belongs (or feeling the need to redeem yourself after a subpar season) is a mentality that is better used as an extra incentive to train hard. In competition, it is always better to fully express your skills and enjoy yourself rather than feel there is a need to prove yourself. You'll be fine if you go out and play like yourself. Be who you are, do what you do, and play how you play. Remind yourself, "This is who I am and what I do every day."

KNOW WHY YOU PLAY

Far too many athletes put far too much emphasis on results and too little on enjoying the moment. Figure skater Peggy Fleming, the women's gold medalist at the 1968 Grenoble Olympics, said, "The first thing is to love your sport. Never do it to please someone else. It has to be yours." If you are playing your sport solely to please someone else, get out of it. Update your life goals and go find more enjoyment or personal meaning doing something else.

Fun is the primary reason to play sports. Ask yourself, "Am I having fun when I train and compete?" If you are not having fun, what are you thinking, feeling, and doing that interferes with thoroughly enjoying your experience? The objective is to have focused fun (not silly fun) in your sport while finding out how great you can play the game. Keep the pleasure and passion in the pursuit.

Jamaican sprinter Usain Bolt is continually gunning for greatness while maintaining a fun-loving approach in competition. This helps him stay free, loose, and athletic at major track meets. In 2012, Bolt became the first man to successfully defend both the 100-meter and 200-meter sprint titles in an Olympic Games. Overall, he sprinted and smiled his way to three gold medals in both Beijing and London (100 meters, 200 meters, and 4 x 100-meter relay). The man with the million-watt smile and signature "To Di World" pose explained, "You have to enjoy yourself [to run your best]."

ACCEPT YOURSELF UNCONDITIONALLY

Sadly, many athletes allow their play to define their worth as a person. This misperception that your value as a person can be measured by how well you play in a particular game underlies many performance and personal problems. Fortunately, your worth is *never* on the line. You are more than the sum of your performance outcomes, so do not feel bad or guilty if you do your best.

Tell yourself that whatever the outcome of a competition, you will always appreciate yourself and feel good about making your best effort. "A gold medal is a wonderful thing, but if you're not enough without it, you'll never be enough with it," explains John Candy's character in the movie *Cool Runnings*. Having unconditional self-acceptance will move you closer to your goals because you will be in the ideal state of mind to succeed. Bottom line: Rate your performance, do not judge yourself.

NEVER STOP TRAINING, NEVER STOP LEARNING

Enjoy the fruits of your labor, but keep working hard on your game. Always seek to improve, even when you are the best at what you do. Be a lifelong learner; make continuous improvement and never-ending development of your gold standard. Embrace the Zen idea of "always a student." That is, even the master realizes that she can become more skilled in the things at which she already excels. A willingness to learn and evolve is invaluable when it comes to attaining personal excellence and achieving peak performance.

"Always a student" is an attitude synonymous with having the growth mind-set that world-renowned Stanford University psychologist Carol Dweck defines in her book *Mindset: The New Psychology of Success*. Specifically, a growth mind-set is one in which you recognize that you have talents that can be enhanced through dedication. A fixed mind-set, on the other hand, is one in which you see your talents as traits that cannot be developed. Achieve more success and happiness in your sport by understanding that you can progress in every area of your performance.

Edwin Moses is a prime example of the growth mind-set. He was a steadfast student of his event throughout his phenomenal track career. Moses won gold medals in the 400-meter hurdles at the 1976 and 1984 Olympics—he was unable to compete in 1980 because of the United States' boycott of the Moscow Games. From 1977 to 1987, Moses won an astounding 107 consecutive finals and set the world record in his event four times. "I always had to keep improving my skills in order to remain competitive and keep winning," said Moses. He further explained, "I think most of [success] is really mental, because I ran against a lot of individuals who were probably more physically talented. But I was able to outsmart them and outthink them and outprepare them."

CONTROL WHAT YOU CAN

The Serenity Prayer by American theologian Reinhold Niebuhr is a valuable tool to add to your mental game toolbox. It's easy to find online and addresses the issue of what we can and can't change. To go a step further, it is good to recognize in sport and life that *most* things cannot be changed.

Learning to emotionally detach from things that cannot be changed, rather than getting distracted by them, can help you stay in the right mind-set. Take the judgment out of it. "It is what it is," as Tiger Woods often says.

Do not allow "uncontrollables" to affect your mentality during game play. This will not only help improve your own performance, but it will also give you the competitive edge over opponents who do not adjust to the same adverse factors and become distracted and stressed as a result.

The only thing an athlete has control over is his or her game. The main things that cannot be controlled in sports include the following:

- Past/future

- Field conditions

- Weather

- Teammates

- Coaches

- Opponents
- Officials
- Spectators
- Media
- Bounce of the ball
- Game schedule
- Importance of the game

MAINTAIN A GREAT PERSPECTIVE

Take your sport seriously, but not so seriously that you completely lose perspective after a tough loss or when things are not going as well as expected. Realize that one's perspective is their reality. So, always keep your participation in its proper place by developing and maintaining a healthy outlook, and never live or die by your sport. Keep your eye on the big picture of life and you'll take the sting out of disappointment and turn it into determination.

Shannon Miller is the most decorated U.S. gymnast ever. She won a combined total of 16 World Championship and Olympic medals and was a member of the gold-medal-winning Magnificent Seven team at the 1996 Atlanta Olympics. Miller was able to maintain a great perspective throughout her stellar career. She said, "I think it's really important to look at the big picture instead of one competition."

Restore a proper perspective as necessary by reminding yourself, "This is just one performance, not my whole career," or "It's only a race (or game, or tryout), not my whole life." The fate of the whole universe does not hinge on the outcome of your next round, match, or game. Losing or underperforming is always disappointing, but it needn't be debilitating.

Sheila Taormina is the only woman to compete in three different sports during Olympic competition. She won a gold medal in the 4x200-meter swim freestyle relay at the 1996 Atlanta Olympics, finished 23rd in the triathlon at the 2004 Athens Olympics, and finished 19th in the modern pentathlon at the 2008 Beijing Olympics. Taormina shared with me how she uses prayer for perspective to manage stress in competition. She explained:

> I always read the Bible and prayed to put sport performance in perspective. I prayed for health of family, friends, and also for people in the world whom I felt were suffering and for whom my race would not relieve their circumstance/condition. This is how I not only relieved sports-performance pressure but also how I fully wanted to remember that my race was not the center of the universe. It was a blessing to have the opportunities I had; therefore, I also believed in racing with a spirit of bravery and not one of fear. Between every pistol shot at the Beijing Olympics, when there was approximately 30 seconds before the command to load for the next shot, I prayed Ephesians 6:10–18.

CHAMPIONS WIN BY NOT DEFEATING THEMSELVES

Achieving success in sports or reaching your fitness goals is hard enough. Don't make it harder by being overly self-critical (about your progress, your appearance, etc.) or by believing that you are not good enough, especially when you are already doing your best. Get off your own back and out of your own way, so to speak.

After all, if a close friend or good teammate was not playing well or was dealing with difficulties, you would encourage, not criticize, him or her. So do the same for yourself by being your best friend on and off the field—no double standards allowed. If you are kind to others but cruel to yourself, practice the reverse of the Golden Rule: One should treat oneself as one would treat others!

HAVE THE ATTITUDE OF A SEASON TICKET HOLDER

A casual fan is loosely involved with his or her team, whereas a season ticket holder or die-hard fan is committed and shows a great deal of passion. A casual fan might boo his or team when things are not going well, but a season ticket holder will still cheer the team on no matter what.

Don't be a casual or fair-weather fan in your own game and life. As a player, remember to also be a good fan by always staying upbeat about what you know and what you can do, whether you happen to be on a hot streak or after a tough loss.

Be emotionally invested in and actively rooting for your own team as well. These are the performers you should also rally around—be a great source of positive support to your teammates for every competition for the whole season, every season.

PROFESSIONALISM WINS THE DAY

Enthusiasm is needed to pump yourself up, especially when you are feeling drained or behind in the game. However, showboating or gloating is a real turnoff to others because of how clownish and amateurish it can look. Like many football announcers say, "When you score a touchdown, act like you've been there before."

Unprofessional behavior often results in costly penalties and change momentum in favor of the opponent.

Pete Sampras won 14 Grand Slam singles titles during his 14-year ATP Tour career, including seven Wimbledon singles titles. Nicknamed the "King of Swing," Sampras was a class act when he played. He explained, "I let my racket do the talking. That's what I am all about, really. I just go out and win tennis matches."

Martial arts master Bruce Lee once stated that "knowledge will give you power, but character will give you respect."Always strive to present yourself in your best light. This is especially important to remember when you are struggling in your game or your team is dealing with adversity. Have respect for yourself and others. Abide by the game's etiquette and rules. Everything you do on and off the field reveals your character. Make sure to always conduct yourself accordingly.

Here's how *not* to act on the field:

- Sulking/whining
- Yelling/screaming
- Breaking the rules
- Throwing or kicking things
- Being rude or snubbing others
- Coasting or going through the motions
- Celebrating in an exaggerated way after *every* basket, shot, or tackle

GET COMFORTABLE BEING UNCOMFORTABLE

Our society has conditioned us to believe there should be no discomfort in life, and when we are uncomfortable, we think something is terribly wrong. As such, we all tend to resist that which is initially uncomfortable. Instead, something is terribly *right* when we are being challenged to grow stronger. The discomfort we feel when we exercise is an important part of the strengthening process. When we're learning something new, like a swing change in golf or the playbook in football, we may feel stressed, frustrated, and uncomfortable, but this does not mean that something is wrong or amiss. Our goal right now is to "get comfortable being uncomfortable," as renowned sports psychologist Ken Ravizza suggests, rather than becoming pessimistic, negative, or hopeless, believing that feelings will never improve.

PEAK PERFORMANCE AND A PILE OF SAND

Achieving peak performance in sports is like trying to keep a small pile of sand from slipping from your grip. If you hold it too tightly, the sand will be squeezed out between your fingers. Likewise, if you hold it too loosely, the sand will slip through your grip. Holding the sand too tightly is analogous to caring too much about the outcome and trying too hard to achieve a result. Holding it too loosely is akin to caring too little and not being mentally disciplined. Most athletes would benefit from caring enough but not caring too much about the outcome in major competitions, so that they can let their talent be natural and unrestrained. "He who grasps loses," wrote Lao-tzu in the *Tao Te Ching*.

POLISH THE ROCK, SHARPEN THE SWORD

They say that writing is an endless process of rewriting. Likewise, sports are an endless process of fine-tuning your athletic skills. Keep looking for further revisions in your mental and physical games. As you progress as an athlete, work toward increasing the quality of your effort while sticking to your training schedule with as few interruptions as possible. This requires deliberately working on the right things at practice with your full focus in the present moment.

Perhaps you've heard the saying "garbage in, garbage out" (GIGO). To perform at a champion's level, transform GIGO into "gold in, gold out." The quality of your work in practice (input) determines your performance in competition (output). Just remember that it's not about how much practice time you put *in;* it's about what you put *into* the practice time.

The most important thing is that you think of each training session as an opportunity to buff up your body and mind—polish the rock, sharpen the sword—to shine on the field. Under the leadership of Vince Lombardi, the Green Bay Packers were the top American football team of the 1960s, winning five world championships over a 7-year span. Lombardi told his players, "We are going to relentlessly chase perfection, knowing full well we will not catch it, because nothing is perfect. But we are going to relentlessly chase it, because in the process we will catch excellence." Now, that's the way to conduct your athletic career!

Relentlessly chase gold in your game with regard to improving your mental and physical strengths, as well as your technical and tactical know-how. Los Angeles Lakers shooting guard Kobe Bryant is a five-time NBA champion. In his book *Kobe Bryant: Hard to the Hoop,* Mark Stewart shares Bryant's thoughts about pushing for perfection: "I'm chasing perfection . . . and if I don't get it, I'm going to get *this* close." Strive to get 1 percent closer to perfection in your own game each day, then let your training come out naturally and unrestrained in competition. Adhere to the seven *P*s: Proper Practice and Preparation Promotes Personal Peak Performance!

GOOD, BETTER, BEST IS YOUR RIGHT ROUTE

How can you objectively evaluate your progress and build on your success? As a mechanism for sparking creativity and generating new ideas for improving your performance, debrief your game play on a regular basis. Evaluate the mental, technical, and tactical aspects. Specifically, ask yourself three questions: 1) What did I do that was *good*? 2) What needs to get *better*? 3) What changes should I make to become my *best*? This process will allow you to think broadly about each area of your game and then drill down to the details. Make this your Champion Journal.

After asking yourself these three questions and recording your responses (ideally, within 24 to 48 hours of your performance), examine what's not working for you and decide what to do differently. The point is to give yourself credit when credit is due and to start working on the right things in practice so that you can take your game to the next level. Learn from mistakes so you don't repeat the same mistakes (e.g., take a mistake you made, rewind it in your mind, and then visualize making the proper play). Review your journal periodically to track your progress.

Opposite is a sample Champion Journal entry for "Mentality" from a professional baseball player. As we've learned from principles like "Stay Strong in Self-Belief" and "Prime Time Is All the Time," champions transcend the mediocrity of the average athlete in how

COMPETITION:
9/7 GAME AGAINST THE YANKEES

What did I do that was good?

- On deck, I visualized getting my pitch and driving it into the left-center or right-center gap.

- I had quality at-bats by following my routine and making adjustments.

- I focused on breathing evenly and deeply to stay free and loose.

What needs to get better?

- Refocus faster after making an error in the field.

What changes should I make to become my best?

- After making an error, tell myself to snap back to the present moment. Focus forward.

- Write "Snap back!" on my glove for use as a positive reminder.

- Want the ball. Think, "Hit it to me."

they understand themselves and view the game. When the odds are stacked against you, are you going to stay strong in a self-belief similar to what Jim Craig of "Miracle on Ice" fame displayed against the Russians? Will you, like Michael Jordan, learn from superficial and temporary failures and keep shooting the ball until you succeed? Are you moving toward developing productive rivalries? These lessons reveal how the best athletes think and tick, so don't forget to bring these insights along with you to the playing field.

CHAPTER FIVE

EXERCISE, NUTRITION, PAIN, INJURIES, AND REGENERATION

We are what we repeatedly do.
Excellence, then, is not an act, but a habit.

—ARISTOTLE

What do exercise adherence, balanced eating, pain management, handling injuries, and regeneration all have in common? They are crucial facets of sports performance that do not typically receive their due care and attention by athletes. This chapter offers valuable ways to deepen your awareness and increase your understanding of these mental challenges. In addition, practical strategies for each subject are provided so that you will be armed with a carefully devised plan of action for success.

CREATE AND SUSTAIN A WINNING STRATEGY FOR YOUR FITNESS

Eighty percent of success is showing up.

—WOODY ALLEN

All of us appreciate that exercise is not just for good physical health. Research has clearly demonstrated that exercise also has a positive impact on mental health. Any type of physical activity is better than no physical activity, because fundamentally there is an athlete existing in all of us. The human body is meant to move!

Whether you are a weekend warrior or a professional athlete, it is important to create and sustain a winning strategy for maintaining your fitness level. Have an "always in season" attitude by staying in shape and taking care of yourself away from the field. For serious athletes, dedication to your workout regimen and a healthy diet will keep you in peak physical condition year-round.

A personal trainer can help you develop the right workout plan to meet your fitness goals. Mark Verstegen, an internationally recognized leader and innovator in the world of athletic-performance training, has authored several trailblazing fitness books: *Core Performance, Core Performance Essentials, Core Performance Endurance, Core Performance Golf,* and *Core Performance Women.* Specifically, each easy-to-follow book is packed with key exercises and clear-cut illustrations accompanying the text.

Check out Verstegen's website www.coreperformance.com for the latest essential information about proactive wellness. Receive expert tips, tracking and reports, a nutrition plan, and personalized training. Many athletes at all levels that I provide consultation to have told me they enjoy reading the educational blog covering popular topics such as nutrition, injury prevention, and sports performance.

Michael Boyle is another great fitness resource. He is one of the foremost experts in the fields of strength and conditioning, performance enhancement, and general fitness. He has served as the head strength and conditioning coach at Boston University, and in that same capacity for the Boston Bruins of the National Hockey League and the 1998 U.S. women's Olympic ice hockey team.

In a 2012 interview for my *Psychology Today* blog (*Trust the Talent*), Boyle shared several noteworthy insights into winning using mind and muscle for athletic success. Specifically, he described an intelligent approach for achieving one's fitness goals, expressing his personal views on burnout prevention and much more. For Boyle, one major area of emphasis is learning how to make slow, steady progress over the long haul. As he explained:

> I think the most common misconception is that it is so hard. It goes back to the tortoise and the hare. Slow and steady wins the race. By slow and steady I don't mean training slow, but progressing slow. Think about this. Start in week one with an empty 45 lb in the bench press and do 10 reps. Add 5 lbs per week for one year. That's just 2.5 lbs on each side of the bar. If you didn't miss a week you would bench press 305 x 10 (52 x 5 = 260; 260 + 45 = 305). To be honest, that is impossible. You would plateau. However, most people are in such a hurry they plateau in a few weeks.

Let's change gears and discuss the critical topic of exercise adherence, because you need to build your body to handle the rigors of participating in a grueling sport or playing all the way through a long season. Here now are several key ingredients you can mix into a champion-level recipe to help you become a workout warrior and stay loyal to your training or fitness regimen.

Train with purpose and passion. You have to be crystal clear about your purpose, your passion, and your mission. Add a little more energy and enthusiasm to each routine. Get rid of a sense of entitlement. Earn your sports or fitness goals by working hard and intelligently every day at the gym. Keep in mind the adage that "Hard work always beats talent when talent doesn't work hard."

Achieve victory through variety. Exercise variety keeps your body running smoothly and your motivation level high. How can you keep your workouts fun and fresh? Experiment with mixed martial arts (MMA) training, kettlebell exercises, hurdle or chute drills, medicine ball situps, and so on. A diversity of exercises will ensure effective and enjoyable workout results.

You are worth the time it takes to exercise. Lack of perceived time is the main reason people give for not exercising on a regular basis. Keep in mind that we all start with the same 168 hours every week. We all have time to do a full workout or an abbreviated workout at home in the morning or at night on days when that is all we have time for or can manage physically. It is always better to commit to doing something rather than just deciding to do nothing.

Find workout partners for support and encouragement. An exercise partner can help keep your training on target. Pledge to meet at the track, pool, or gym on set days and times. Make sure to push each other during the workout. This arrangement makes it harder to skip the workout because your "goal buddy" depends on you to show up. You've both scheduled the workout. No matter what happens in your day, try your best to adhere strictly to this regular workout schedule with your partner.

Break down the workout into manageable chunks. This strategy can help keep you from feeling overwhelmed. Focus squarely on each segment and only that segment at one time. Don't worry about the second half of your exercise routine when you're just warming up. This principle also applies to performance. For instance, you can break a marathon down into two 10-mile runs and then a 10-K run to the finish. For a beginning runner, you can reframe a 5-K as only jogging one mile three times (plus a little extra).

Keep an exercise log and a workout calendar. Each month, keep track of the total number of workouts you've completed. Place a gold dot in your exercise log or on your calendar for each day you performed your workout as planned. This symbol will be visual proof of the excellence you want to achieve and also inspire you to keep working toward your fitness goals. Include a weekly calendar of scheduled workouts for planning purposes as well.

Take full responsibility for your own health and fitness. When you modify your language from "I'll try" or "Maybe" to "I will" and "I'm going to," you transform your behavior. Motivation will always fluctuate, but it is irrelevant at the moment of truth, when you actually act. So act as if you are motivated—that is, increase your "motive-action"—to keep your feet moving forward and defeat any potential resistance, whether that resistance is mental or physical. You'll discover that full motivation usually shows up during a good workout, not beforehand.

Treat yourself like a champion. Regular exercise will make you feel more alive and much better about yourself. Show up at the track, pool, or gym, and take pleasure in the endorphin rush you feel. Enjoy the experience. Afterward you'll feel as good as gold. In fact, regular exercise is one of the best gifts you can ever give yourself because of all the mental and physical benefits. So stick to your exercise regimen until it becomes your personal way of life.

EAT FOR PLEASURE
AND FOR PERFORMANCE

The wise man should consider that health
is the greatest of human blessings.

Let food be your medicine.

—HIPPOCRATES

The importance of proper nutrition for sports-performance enhancement and quality of life cannot be overstated. "Your body is a temple, but only if you treat it as one" is good food for thought. Take care of your temple, and your temple will take care of you. Taking these precise actions will also keep you more energized, alert, and focused on your training and performance goals. No one can concentrate very well on daily activities or excel in training when hungry or dehydrated.

Dr. Jose Antonio is CEO of the International Society of Sports Nutrition. I asked him to give me the elevator speech he delivers to serious athletes. Here's Antonio's advice:

> Proper sports nutrition and supplementation is critical for improving body composition and performance when coupled with an intense exercise training program. Athletes should strive for "progress, not perfection" when it comes to sports nutrition. Emphasis on eating lean meats, healthy fats, and unprocessed carbohydrates is key. Also, the use of certain supplements such as creatine, beta-alanine, and protein (especially postworkout) is an effective strategy for enhancing the effects of exercise.

When you think about nutrition, strive to be really mindful in your method. Fully appreciate the importance of developing champion eating habits, so you are eating for both training and enjoyment. Many athletes eat the same thing week in and week out without much careful thought about what they are actually putting in their bodies. Other athletes have a balanced diet, but then chew on autopilot—not truly tasting their food—because they are mentally preoccupied with everything already going on in their very demanding days.

Here are several suggestions for nurturing a more mindful approach to your nutrition and developing a healthier relationship with the food you eat.

Build a winning meal plan. Learn more about sports nutrition and seek out specific suggestions about food choices. A sports nutritionist can help you develop an individualized meal plan that includes a wide variety of foods. Decide in advance what you will pick up at the supermarket each week rather than just choosing food off the top of your head as you're walking from aisle to aisle. Make sure to treat yourself to a junk day (or meal) every now and then.

Bring along balanced snacks. Busy athletes sometimes will binge at night because they did not eat enough during the day. For regular and constant fuel, carry balanced snacks with you, such as nuts, raisins, and bananas. These will help maintain your blood sugar level throughout the day. Keep a water bottle nearby, too.

Take mindful bites and sips. Activate your senses while you're eating meals. Did you smell the aroma of the food being cooked? Do you taste the spices in your food? Do you feel the texture of the food on your tongue? Give your entire attention to what you are eating right now by enjoying each bite. If you notice you are eating too fast, count your bites to help you slow down and think about what you're eating.

Feed your good wolf. In our discussion on self-talk, we put emphasis on not beating yourself up by what you say to yourself. That's important. Feeling guilty about what you just ate is how you feed the Big Bad Wolf, not the good wolf. Instead, if you do decide to eat more of something or perhaps order a favorite dessert, tell yourself it was a clearly thought-out and planned decision, and then thoroughly enjoy eating that favorite item. Then be fully accepting of your choice afterward. Don't ever get down on yourself for what you just ate.

Neutralize environmental effects. Our eating behaviors are often subconsciously and significantly influenced by the environment around us. We will eat more quickly when there is blaring music, when the television is on, or when our dining companions are fast eaters. Being aware of the factors that can influence your eating behavior will help you learn how to take your time when it is time to eat and enjoy eating more because you are in control of your eating patterns.

Avoid disordered eating. Scores of athletes develop a preoccupation with weight, body size and shape, and the specific aspects of their appearance, especially in judged sports like gymnastics and ice skating, sports with revealing uniforms like diving and swimming, endurance sports like cross-country, and sports with weight categories like wrestling. Other factors that contribute to risk for an athlete include dieting at an early age and perfectionistic personality traits.

Obsessing over caloric intake and calories burned via the amount of exercise you're doing is part of a problem, not the route to a solution. Seek professional guidance immediately if you notice this kind of thinking (and restrictive or binge-eating behaviors) because of the possibility of greater injury, impaired growth and mental functioning, and serious health risks, including osteoporosis. Besides, it's not about what you're eating, it's what's eating you that you need to tackle. Nip any such concerns in the bud before they blossom into bigger issues that are much harder to handle.

Fill your tank with top racing fuel. Think of your body as a NASCAR racing car built for peak performance. Fill your gas tank with top racing fuel for maximum power and speed on the day of the competition. What you put into your body is what will determine your performance on the field. This is not the time to make new food choices: Don't try a new power bar or a different energy drink, as they can upset your stomach. Experiment with new food and drinks only before practices, not games.

PAIN MANAGEMENT: BRAIN OVER PAIN

It only hurt once . . . from beginning to end.

—JAMES COUNSILMAN, AFTER SWIMMING THE ENGLISH CHANNEL AT AGE 58

In any sport or exercise routine, much of your success depends on how well you handle noninjury pain, soreness, tiredness, and discomfort. Bodily aches and pains are a necessary part of improving and growing your performance. They are a key part of the training process. Jackie Joyner-Kersee, a three-time Olympic gold medalist, explained it very well. "Ask any athlete: We all hurt at times. I'm asking my body to go through seven different tasks. To ask it not to ache would be too much."

Allen Iverson, a former Philadelphia 76ers all-star guard, is mentioned as the "greatest little man to ever play the game," along with little superplayers Bob Cousy and Nate Archibald. Barely 6 feet tall and weighing just 165 pounds, Iverson was one of the legitimate tough guys in the NBA. "I'm used to being banged up," he would say. "You try to suck it up and not think about it. You just play off your adrenaline."

Perhaps the most important point to understand here is that

intense discomfort is often the price tag for personal greatness. Most very intense physical activities, such as wrestling, swimming, cycling, climbing, and running, are to a large extent one big "suffer-fest." Nevertheless, don't ever forget that there is also a wonderful world of pleasure, pride, and satisfaction to be gained from the achieved goals that rest on the other side of pain.

Experiencing extreme fatigue during the final miles of a race is known as "hitting the wall" in running or "bonking" in cycling. As long as you are not damaging your health or risking (or aggravating) an injury, you just have to learn to dig deep and find that last high gear to move into so you can motor through the wall or beat the bonk. Ann Trason, an American ultramarathon runner who has set twenty world records during her career, said, "It hurts up to a point and then it doesn't get any worse."

The Olympic triathlon (swim 1.5 kilometers, bike 40 kilometers, run 10 kilometers) made its debut in the 2000 Sydney Games. American Susan Williams placed third with an impressive total time of 2:05:08 at the second Olympic triathlon in Athens in 2004; she is the only U.S. triathlete to have earned a spot on the Olympic podium in the sport. In a 2012 interview with Susan for my *Trust the Talent* blog, she shared how she handled noninjury pain when training and during competition:

> From a background in swimming, I knew that you get better by working hard. In training, I wouldn't hold back, because I wanted to be the best I could be. In competition, I wanted to walk away from the race knowing that I did my very best. If I backed down, I knew that I would feel very unsatisfied with the race and be very down on myself.

In his memoir, *What I Talk About When I Talk About Running*, best-selling Japanese novelist Haruki Murakami argues that talent is nothing without focus and endurance. He also shares the extreme mantra he successfully used during a 62-mile ultramarathon: "I'm not human. I'm a piece of machinery. I don't need to feel a thing. Just forge on ahead."

Several techniques can help you increase your pain tolerance, move through pain, and maybe even accept it. However, with an illness or injury (sharp pain, a concussion, torn ligaments), you have to shut down early and live to train and win another day.

Always consult your sports medicine team about any injury questions or concerns—especially concerning concussions. Immediate Post-Concussion Assessment and Cognitive Testing (ImPACT) is the gold standard for concussion diagnosis and evaluation. Please visit www.impacttest.com for important information about concussion awareness and management. A few key features found on this site include common signs and symptoms of a concussion, important research/publications, and doctor referrals.

The tactics provided here are intended to help you deal with pain or discomfort during physical exertion and should never be used to ignore underlying health problems, further injure yourself, or mask a preexisting condition or injury so that you go from bad to worse. Talk with your coaches and sports medicine team to make intelligent and informed decisions about injury prevention and treatment. Always keep in mind your long-term athletic goals.

The key to moving through soreness and discomfort is finding a method that is both personal and meaningful for you and your sport. Push through fatigue and find that extra gear. Get your second wind and stay on pace.

Subsequently, make sure to balance a grueling workout or race with plenty of rest and recovery. Here are several positive pain-management strategies for peak performance and maximum endurance.

Monitor your body's response during exertion. Periodically check in with your body and the current pace you are going in order to make appropriate adjustments. Scan your body from head to toe for tension and relax tight areas. Keep your shoulders free of tension.

Self-reflection is needed: Ask yourself, "Am I going too fast/slow to achieve maximum results?" "Am I maintaining proper technique, especially when I'm fatigued?" "Am I refueling throughout vigorous activity to avoid depleting glycogen stores and crashing and burning as a result?"

In the marathon world, experienced runners constantly warn novices not to go out too fast in their excitement to take part after months of anticipation and hard training. A rookie's prerace plan can fly out the window and novices end up hitting the wall and hitting it hard. The mantra is to "always stick to the prerace plan."

Put your attention on what feels good. While exercising, it is always better to focus on the joy of movement, maintaining correct form, and good breathing rather than on the burning sensation in your legs or arms, especially at the start or end of your workout.

One elite runner shared with me his strategy. He focuses on his eyelids while he runs 400-meter repeats in practice. He smiled when I asked him why he does that and then explained, "My eyelids are the only part of my entire body that doesn't hurt when I run 400s." An endurance athlete shared with me that the act of smiling during a rough patch of a race helps her release pain and feel more joyful.

Shift negative thoughts to positive thoughts. Negative thoughts ("This hurts," "I don't want to do this") will slow you down and increase muscle tightness, which intensifies the sensation of pain. During a rough patch, put a smile on your face and repeat a positive phrase over and over, such as "Stay strong," "Get tough," "Earn it," "Light and quick," or "Relax and roll."

Embrace the suck. This is a U.S. military training stance that you can adopt. It means accept the discomfort that comes from working hard and pushing past perceived limits. Accept the challenge. Enjoy the struggle.

Listen to your favorite music. Music can put you in a great mood and be a good distraction from discomfort for the duration of the workout. Periodically add new songs to your running/gym playlist to prevent your tunes from becoming stale and repetitive. But at the same time, keep your favorites in the mix, as they can be inspiring to listen to again and again and be good reminders of success.

Practice metaphorical imagery to minimize the sensation of pain. For example, a swimmer may visualize the pain washing over her and then see herself leaving that pain behind in her wake in the water. A runner may picture himself as a powerful tank that cannot be slowed or stopped when going forward.

Focus on accomplishing your task. Focus all your energy on execution of your sport and everything else will melt away, including pain. George Foreman, an Olympic gold medalist and two-time world heavyweight boxing champion, explained, "If I see what I want real good in my mind, I don't notice any pain in getting it."

Do what you can do in this single moment. Dave Scott, a six-time Ironman triathlon world champion, would repeat to himself during competition, "Do what I can do in this moment." That is, stay positive and do your best in the here and now. Use Scott's mantra for your own races and training efforts. It can help.

The more adept you become at these techniques for building mental stamina, the less likely you will be to let pain hinder your aspiration—whether it is achieving a particular fitness goal, winning a competition, scaling a mountain, or simply enjoying your sport to the ultimate level. If you can learn how to actually move through the pain you feel, excellence awaits.

USE YOUR HEAD
WHEN YOU'RE INJURED

Adversity introduces a man to himself.

—ANONYMOUS

Unfortunately, a sports injury is a common challenge for all types of athletes. Sports injuries are classified as either traumatic (hard contact) or overuse (repetitive stress). The best way to prevent injuries is to maintain excellent physical conditioning (build a strong base during the off-season), stick to a sound warmup routine, work on the proper technique, sharpen all of your mental skills, and dial down your stress levels.

Under personal or professional stress, muscle tension will increase, and attention will decrease, producing reduced situational awareness. Thus, you are more likely to miss clues in the environment and experience delayed reaction times. You can lessen the likelihood of injury on the field by managing your life stress off the field.

New England Patriots quarterback Tom Brady suffered a season-ending knee injury—anterior cruciate ligament (ACL) and medial collateral ligament (MCL) tears in his left knee—in the first game of the 2008 NFL season. However, he returned to the field in 2009 and played solidly once again as if he had not missed a beat. Rather than fret about his reconstructed knee, Brady instead focused on throwing touchdowns. Indeed, Brady was named AFC offensive player of the week for his performance in the season opener, a 25–24 win over the Buffalo Bills.

In 2011, St. Louis Cardinals' slugger Albert Pujols fractured his left wrist and forearm after a collision at first base while playing against the Kansas City Royals. He was able to return to the team much earlier than was anticipated. Less than 2 months after the injury, Pujols blasted the longest home run recorded to that point at Busch Stadium in St. Louis, estimated at 465 feet.

A wild card entry, the Cardinals advanced to the playoffs on the final day of the season and proceeded to beat the Philadelphia Phillies and the Milwaukee Brewers en route to the World Series. St. Louis then defeated the Texas Rangers in seven games to complete their thrilling title run.

Major ligament tears are no longer the automatic career-altering injuries they were just a few decades ago. NBA all-star power forward Blake Griffin, MLB all-star outfielder Andre Ethier, NFL All-Pro running back Adrian Peterson, and UFC welterweight champion Georges St-Pierre have all returned to top form in recent years with surgically repaired knees. St-Pierre spent 19 months away from competition after undergoing surgery and an extensive rehabilitation process following a torn ACL in his right knee. In the main event of UFC 154 in Montreal on November 17, 2012, he made a triumphant return to the octagon by grinding out a thrilling five-round unanimous decision over Carlos Condit to reclaim his belt.

Overcoming the emotional and physical challenges of a moderate or major injury requires the ability to deal effectively with the mental side of rehabilitation. The mental side is especially challenging because in addition to the physical pain the athlete must deal with, there is the emotional pain of being temporarily sidelined and not being able to perform at preinjury levels.

The goal for the any athlete is to be master of the injury rather than letting the injury master the athlete. Bring your champion's mind-set to the training room and make rehab your new sport until you get your game back, and you will get that game back. Here are several tips for how you can be a winner in the inner game of rehab, so you can make a triumphant return to the field.

Know and understand the five stages of loss. There are several common stages people often—but not always—go through following a significant injury. The first stage is shock or denial ("I can't believe this is happening"). The second stage is anger ("Why now?" "This isn't fair!"). The third stage is bargaining ("If only . . ."). The fourth stage is depression ("Rehab is useless; why even bother?"). The fifth stage is acceptance ("This didn't happen for the best, but I will make the best of what did happen").

Team up for motivation and support. For example, seek assistance from medical professionals and get encouragement from family, friends, and teammates. The key is to talk about your feelings rather than keeping them to yourself. Don't be too proud to talk with a counselor, if needed. Rehabilitation is an individual process, different for everyone, but that does not mean you have to do rehab all alone.

Patience is the prescription. Be incredibly patient, but also persistent, especially during a long, slow recovery process. If you underdo your rehabilitation, you will only prolong your recovery. If you overdo your rehabilitation, then you might reinjure yourself quickly and make the outcome even worse. Adhere to the recommendations of your athletic trainers and medical doctors. In other words, let the experts be the experts whenever you ask questions or express your concerns along the way. Trust the process to deliver the results you want as a person and an athlete, and it likely will.

Fire up your imagination. Spend a few minutes each and every day visualizing the injured area healing, becoming stronger, and returning to normal. Imagine an ice pack or healing colors surrounding the injured area when you experience pain from the injury. Spend some time studying game films or imagining yourself performing your sports skills each day. That will keep your mental athletic abilities sharp as you wait for your physical abilities to return.

Diver Laura Wilkinson broke three bones in her foot during

final training for the 2000 U.S. Olympic trials. Unable to dive for 2 months during her recovery, Wilkinson visualized ripping her dives each day. Not only did Wilkinson qualify for the Olympics, she won a gold medal in Sydney even though her foot was not fully healed.

Spin a negative into a positive. In collaboration with your sports medicine team, discover creative ways to make the most of your recovery time through exercise or by pursuing hobbies or other interests. If you injured your lower body, strengthen your upper body by lifting weights or using a hand ergometer. If you injured your upper body, strengthen your lower body by lifting weights or using a stationary bike. Maintain good self-care habits by getting plenty of rest and sleep, and continue to maintain good balanced eating.

Power through plateaus and setbacks. Embrace the attitude that any setback is an opportunity for a comeback. Stay optimistic during any downturns or plateaus in the recovery process. Recovery does not happen overnight or even occur in a straight line. Anticipate waves and ups and downs and remember these are all part of the healing process. Keep on keeping on!

Let's close out this section by imagining a scenario in which a student-athlete has recently been sidelined with, say, a grade III ankle sprain. How can a champion respond in a challenging situation such as this one and win the rehab game? The student-athlete can be a champion by making rehab her new sport until she gets her game back. In other words, she should approach the recovery process like any other athletic challenge and take it head-on without giving way to fear and doubt.

Specifically, she should bring her best effort and attitude to the training room instead of the playing field; adhere to the recovery plan that she develops with her athletic trainers and doctors; hit the books hard and excel in the classroom; talk with family, friends, coaches, and teammates and get their support; get plenty of rest and sleep to facilitate the healing process; and visualize herself on the field again with her teammates and mentally practice running through the same drills they're actually doing. Taking these power steps will ensure that she makes a confident return to game action after receiving the thumbs-up to play from her sports medicine team.

REGENERATION: RELAX YOUR BODY SO YOU CAN TAX YOUR BODY

Relaxation means releasing all concern and tension and letting the natural order of life flow through one's being.
—DONALD CURTIS, NOTED AUTHOR AND LECTURER

A champion understands that regeneration is one key to sustainable success. One needs to relax mentally and to allow the body to rest and recover from hard training. Think of regeneration as the yin to training's yang. Burning the candle at both ends by overtraining and insufficient recovery results in burnout and increases the risk of injury and illness. When you're tired, your ability to play productively and think clearly is compromised. NFL coaching legend Vince Lombardi cautioned, "Fatigue makes cowards of us all."

Relaxation training is a necessary component of regeneration, and it is especially important for counterbalancing the wear and tear of playing through a long season. Discover which relaxation techniques work best for you to diminish physical exhaustion and mental weariness. Practicing deep relaxation on a daily basis will help you quiet your mind and keep physical tension at a minimum. Heed these words by the ancient Chinese philosopher Lao-tzu: "Deal with the small before it becomes large." Strive to release stress and tension as soon as you notice it is beginning to build.

Recharge your mind and body with deep relaxation. In addition to using a 15-second centering breath (see page 48), experiment with a variety of other approaches. For example, incorporate mental imagery for deep relaxation. Recline in your favorite chair at home or lie down on a bench in the locker room before practice and breathe slowly and deeply for 10 minutes while imagining that your body is floating in space or in a hot tub. Make sure to turn off your cell phone. Simply enjoy the beauty of silence, and let your mind clear of fog.

Take some time to decompress, to get away from the sport, and then get back to training. Try having an occasional rest day that has no purpose or goal other than letting your body rest and rejuvenate! Also, make room in your schedule for some lighthearted activities. What do you enjoy doing in your spare time? What are your favorite hobbies and interests? Aim to relax your body away from training so that you can tax your body in training. To perform at a champion's level, commit to being fully rested and ready for all of your practices and games (see Appendix B for sleep tips).

Nap for peak performance. Imagine that one day your head is drowsy and your feet are dragging—perhaps you did not get a full night's sleep. But there isn't much time for slack and you still have a full day's activities ahead of you, including your workout at the gym. To nap or not to nap, that seems to be the question. But if you do decide to take an afternoon nap, how long should it be? Is a longer nap always better?

Findings from a 2006 research study by Australian psychologists Amber Brooks and Leon Lack suggest that a 10-minute afternoon nap for participants restricted to about 5 hours of sleep is the most recuperative length of nap (for increased cognitive performance, vigor, and wakefulness) in comparison to either no nap or naps of precisely 5, 20, and 30 minutes. Be sure to consider these facts while you discover your own magic number. Remember that naps really do help on those occasions when you are tired and need a quick, chemical-free performance boost.

Try Progressive Muscle Relaxation (PMR). This is a powerful and popular technique for achieving deep relaxation. PMR involves systematically alternating between tensing and relaxing various muscle groups throughout your body one at a time. Tightening and relaxing a muscle makes the muscle more relaxed than it was beforehand. Being able to control muscle tension requires great self-awareness, so, while improving your ability to focus, this exercise will also help you notice the difference between the contrasting sensations of tension and relaxation.

The key is to contract each muscle group to about 50 percent tension—not so hard that you hurt yourself, but enough so you can feel it. Hold each contraction for 6 to 8 seconds, then slowly release the contraction to allow the muscles to fully relax. Breathe in slowly and deeply while you tense; breathe out slowly and fully as you release.

Relaxation exercises, whether PMR or body scans (simply focusing on the sensations in each part of your body one area at a time), work best when you begin with the head and work your way down to your toes. Why? The mind is the boss of the body, so if you relax starting at the top, where we hold most of our tension, and move downward (rather than going from the bottom up), the other muscle groups will follow along like dutiful workers. Move slowly down through the body, contracting and relaxing the muscle groups as you go.

Here is a PMR exercise you can use to become less tense mentally and physically. Skip any strained or injured muscle groups (or just *think* relaxation into these areas), and always check first with a doctor before doing this exercise if you have health or injury concerns.

Position yourself by sitting comfortably in a reclining chair or lying down in bed before going to sleep. Prepare for this exercise by wearing loose clothing, dimming or turning off overhead lights, uncrossing your arms and legs, and gently closing your eyes.

Begin by breathing deeply and mindfully for 3 to 5 minutes. Breathe in through the nose and breathe out through the mouth. Inhale relaxation into your body and exhale tension out of your body. Give yourself permission to let go of worries or concerns; you have nothing else to do, no one in particular you have to be, and nowhere else to go.

FOREHEAD: Lift your eyebrows enough to wrinkle your forehead. Hold this tension in your forehead and scalp . . . focus on that tension . . . and release. Allow your forehead to become soft and smooth.

FACE: Tighten the muscles of your face by scrunching your eyes shut, wrinkling your nose, and tightening your cheeks and chin. Hold this tension in your face . . . and release.

SHOULDERS: Raise your shoulders up to your ears and hold. Feel the tension build to a peak . . . and drop your shoulders back down into a comfortable position.

BACK/CHEST: Tighten the muscles of your back by arching your back slightly. Feel your back tightening, pulling your shoulders back and your chest outward. Hold this tension . . . and let go into a comfortable position.

BICEPS/FOREARMS: Tighten both biceps by curling your arms. Squeeze for a few moments more . . . focus on that tension . . . and release.

RIGHT HAND/WRIST: Squeeze your right hand into a fist. Feel the tension in your hand and wrist. Notice the contrast between the tension in your right hand and the relaxation in your left hand. Hold it for a few moments more . . . and release.

LEFT HAND/WRIST: Squeeze your left hand into a fist. Feel the tension in your hand and wrist. Notice the contrast between the tension in your left hand and the relaxation in your right hand. Hold it for a few moments more . . . and release.

LOWER BACK/BUTT: Focus on the muscles of your butt. Tighten these muscles. Hold this tension . . . and release.

THIGHS/SHINS: Tighten all the muscles of your legs by lifting your legs a few inches off the ground (keep them straight), squeezing your thighs, and pointing your toes toward your face so that you can also feel tension in your shins. Focus on this tension . . . and release.

THIGHS/CALVES: Tighten all the muscles of your legs again by lifting your legs a few inches off the ground (keep them straight), squeezing your thighs, and, this time, pointing your toes away from your body so that you can also feel tension in your calves. Focus on this tension . . . and release. Wiggle your toes.

Finally, allow your muscles to become warmer and heavier as you sink into the chair or bed. Enjoy the deep relaxation you are now experiencing as it becomes deeper and deeper. Continue to breathe slowly, deeply, and rhythmically. Keep going if you like by repeating the 10 steps or perhaps targeting any specific muscle groups that require extra attention. Drift off to sleep if you are in bed or continue on with your day, feeling relaxed and refreshed.

In addition to PMR, there are several more effective ways to discharge stress on the spot, including putting a big smile on your face, practicing walking or sitting meditation, shaking the tension from your arms and legs, jumping up and down a few times, splashing cold water on your face, humming a tune, or squeezing a tennis ball to release the tension.

You now have the knowledge and mental tools required to give exercise adherence, balanced eating, pain management, handling injuries, and regeneration their due care and attention. To move forward, fuel your body with the right nutrition for peak performance, adhere to your conditioning program, move through the wall of pain and discomfort and achieve goals that rest on the other side, use your head when you're injured to win the inner game of rehab, and make time for active recovery so you have a fresh mind and a healthy body to finish the season on a high note. As you progress in your sports career, the necessity for staying on top of these issues in order to reach your goals will only increase. Knowing this, can you afford not to stay on top of these facets of your performance by keeping a closer eye on them?

CHAPTER SIX

TAKE CONTROL OF YOUR PERSONAL DESTINY

The destiny of man is in his own soul.

—HERODOTUS

There are many fascinating and important psychological studies that have shed light on the mental side of personal growth, as well as athletic performance and enhancement. In this chapter, you will be introduced to several classic studies, coupled with cutting-edge research from sports psychology as well as other psychology disciplines. For example, you will learn about complementary topics crucial to athletes at all levels, such as the need to avoid groupthink ("Watch Your Asch!"), the significance of deferred gratification ("Can You Pass the Marshmallow Test?"), and the benefits of social facilitation ("Let's Get Social"). You will develop an increased ability to think, feel, and act your way to greatness in sport and life.

WATCH YOUR ASCH!

Studies have shown that conformity in thinking can lead to poor decision making, which can be detrimental to your sports career. As such, it is essential to understand how someone can easily fall into groupthink, and why it is important to think as an individual to perform as a champion. Research psychologist Irving Janis coined the term *groupthink* in 1972, describing it as a "mode of thinking that people engage in . . . when the members' strivings for unanimity override their motivation to realistically appraise alternative courses of action."

In 1951, social psychologist Solomon Asch and his colleagues conducted a study on conformity in groups, using college students as subjects. The subjects were seated in a classroom and were told that they were participating in a vision test. Each subject was placed in a group comprising five to seven "confederates"—subjects aware of the experiment.

For each test, the group was shown a large white card with a single vertical black line on it, followed by a separate card with three vertical black lines of varying lengths—labeled *a*, *b*, and *c*. The group members were asked to identify which of the three lines matched the line on the first card. The group was then shown another set of cards, and this process was repeated for eighteen trials.

The subjects were positioned within the groups to answer toward the end of each trial. During the first two trials, the confederates provided correct answers. However, in 12 of the 18 trials, the confederates were instructed to provide obviously wrong answers. The aim of these trials was to see if the subjects would go along with other group members by agreeing to the wrong answers.

Results of this experiment indicated that the extent of pressure to conform was even greater than what Asch had anticipated. Overall, subjects agreed with the wrong answer provided by the group 37 percent of the time. An astounding 75 percent of the subjects conformed on at least one trial by agreeing with the wrong answer. However, when these same subjects took a written version of the test, they chose the correct answer 98 percent of the time.

Interpretation of these test results clearly demonstrates that people will often choose an answer they know to be wrong simply because other members of the group did so. Subjects chose incorrect answers because they did not want to stand out from the group and risk ridicule. Conformity means going along with other group members, even when the generally held views show poor judgment.

To perform at a champion's level, don't conform by cutting corners with regard to attitude, effort, and striving to be the best athlete possible. Make excellence your gold standard by never settling in the quest toward your best, whether or not this is the case for teammates or your peer group in general. Internally, always compare yourself with other champions and high-performing role models in your approach to training and competition. By doing so, you can take control of your athletic future and your personal destiny.

CAN YOU PASS THE MARSHMALLOW TEST?

In 1972, Stanford psychologist Walter Mischel and his fellow researchers conducted a study on deferred gratification, using children aged 4 to 6 years old as subjects. He offered one marshmallow to each child. He told the children they could eat the treat, but if they waited for 15 minutes before eating it, he would give them another marshmallow. The researchers timed how long each child resisted the temptation to eat the marshmallow, and whether doing so had an effect on his or her future success.

Mischel placed the children in a room empty of distractions and set a marshmallow on a table. Some children ate the marshmallow as soon as the researchers left the room, thus forfeiting the second marshmallow. One-third of the children struggled long enough to get the second marshmallow. The results showed that the older the child, the longer they were able to delay gratification.

The first follow-up study on the same children was conducted in 1988, 16 years later, and yielded remarkable results. Specifically, there existed a positive correlation between the results of the marshmallow test and the success of the children as young adults. The young adults who had shown delayed gratification as children were described by their parents as significantly more competent that their counterparts. In 1990, a second follow-up study showed that the ability to delay gratification also positively correlated with higher SAT scores.

Self-control is a secret of champions. They are willing to delay immediate gratification and tolerate frustration slightly longer for a larger reward. You can pass the marshmallow test in your own sport and life by developing and applying personal delay tactics to stay the course when you're presented with tempting treats. For example, distract yourself with music, deep breathing, or conversation when you're tempted to stray from your nutrition plan. Rather than surrendering to the fleeting impulse to cut your workout short, shout out to yourself, "Go for the gold!" and keep going. Imagine how good you will feel after successfully completing the full workout.

Accept that each day you will be confronted with all sorts of marshmallow tests. Meet each challenge head-on. Waiting is worthwhile, and patience pays. Think more about what you're winning than what you're forgoing. Tell yourself, "I have the willpower to pursue my present goal, regardless of any momentary discomfort." Keep your eyes on the prize and your feet moving forward. Eventually, acting like you're a gold medalist will become second nature. So, how many marshmallow temptations will you resist today?

LET'S GET SOCIAL

Dr. Norman Triplett is now recognized as the grandfather of sports psychology for the pioneering research he conducted in the late 1800s and early 1900s. A psychology professor at Indiana University and an avid cyclist, Triplett was interested in examining how the presence of others impacted an individual's performance in a variety of tasks, including athletic performance.

In 1898, Triplett published his initial findings in a paper titled "The Dynamogenic Factors in Pacemaking and Competition" in the *American Journal of Psychology*. Specifically, he found that cyclists achieve significantly faster times when riding in the presence of pacemakers, or other competitors, than when racing against the clock in solo time trials. Triplett concluded that "the bodily presence of another rider is a stimulus to the racer in arousing the competitive instinct; that another can thus be the means of releasing or freeing nervous energy for him that he cannot of himself release; and, further, that the sight of movement in that other by perhaps suggesting a higher rate of speed, is also an inspiration to greater effort."

In 1924, Floyd Allport coined the term *social facilitation* to describe the tendency that people perform better on simple or well-learned tasks in the presence of others. However, if the task is difficult, the presence of others can have the opposite effect—performance is inhibited as physiological arousal or activation becomes excessive. This helps explain in part why some athletes play better in practice than in games.

How can Triplett's social facilitation findings relate directly to enhancing your own sports performance? Look for opportunities to include others for increasing effort on simple or well-learned tasks. You can take a Spinning class or find a cycling buddy rather than riding alone. You can also bring along an imaginary competitor to compete against when you go on solo rides. Rather than closing practice to spectators, a coach can invite fans to watch the team scrimmage or run through drills.

How can you overcome excessive physiological activation for a complex task like golf? Let's consider a typical golfer warming up before a competitive round. She might be striping the ball on the driving range, but then experiences first-tee jitters in the presence of her playing partners, although the physical requirements of the task are identical. Because she is overexcited and self-conscious as she waits for her turn, she loses the rhythm in her swing and proceeds to slice the ball into the deep rough.

How can our heroine learn to play more effectively in the presence of others? In practice, she can perform jumping jacks for, say, 60 to 90 seconds and then do repetitions hitting shots with an elevated heart rate. This will help her better manage her nerves while on the course and improve her chances of performing well against others. She can also simulate competition by challenging other players to see who can hit shots closest to selected targets.

Our heroine should also develop a good preshot routine, such as the one below, and stick with it on the first tee and throughout her round.

1. Focus on the shot by selecting a precise target.

2. Imagine the ball splitting the fairway.

3. Take one deep breath to quiet the mind and reduce tension.

4. Make one or two rehearsal swings to get the best tempo.

5. Allow the swing to happen.

She gets her mind right first, then her body (steps 2 and 3), then her tempo, and then just swings. Eventually the first tee won't scare her . . . she'll scare the first tee by how well she does!

MEET THE SPORTS PARENTS

Meet the Parents is a hilarious look at familial relationships that features Ben Stiller, Teri Polo, and Robert De Niro at the top of their comedic games. Stiller plays Gaylord "Greg" Focker, a male nurse who plans to ask his girlfriend, Pam Byrnes (Polo), to marry him. De Niro's character, Jack Byrnes, a retired CIA agent, is Pam's tightly wound father. The overprotective future father-in-law soon becomes Greg's worst nightmare.

During a weekend visit to Pam's parents' house, Greg finds himself under the watchful eye of Jack, who is hell-bent on making sure that he will be an honorable and trustworthy husband for Pam. In addition to subjecting Greg to a polygraph test, Jack explains the importance of trustworthiness by sharing his "Circle of Trust." There are only two possible places that people can be: People you trust are on the inside of the circle, while people you don't trust are on the outside of the circle.

The Circle of Trust concept can be valuable in helping parents think about how to best support their son or daughter in athletics. Building trust within a parent-child relationship can be difficult. Parents think they know the best approach for helping their child succeed in sports. However, best intentions can and do often go wrong. It doesn't matter what you think about your advice; it matters what your child thinks about your advice.

Draw a circle on a piece of paper. This is your child's Circle of Trust. A dot inside the circle represents a behavior helpful to your child. A dot outside the circle represents a behavior not helpful to your child. To be a champion sports parent, work with your child to identify whether your behaviors, with regard to his or her sports participation, land inside or outside the circle. Creating a visual representation such as this can be very beneficial during brainstorming efforts and help you make positive and practical changes, as well as bond with your child.

So, what are athletes' usual preferences for parental behavior? In a 2010 study published in the *Journal of Applied Sport Psychology*, Dr. Camilla Knight and her colleagues at the University of Alberta, Canada, surveyed junior tennis players' preferences for parental behavior during competition. Overall, 11 focus groups were conducted with 42 high-performance Canadian tennis players. Major themes identified included:

- Parents should comment on attitude and effort, but refrain from technical and tactical instruction.

- Parents should provide practical advice (e.g., reminders about nutrition and doing warmups).

- Parents' nonverbal signals should match their verbal communication (i.e., making encouraging statements in tandem with relaxed body language and gestures).

- Parents should understand and respect the etiquette of the game (e.g., avoiding displays of bad manners, such as screaming at the officials).

Most athletes across all sports and ages (even pro and Olympic athletes) would readily agree with these themes. Additionally, timing of feedback is particularly important. As a parent, you should avoid giving long lectures or having in-depth discussions about your child's performance on the ride to and from the game or practice. The dinner table is also not an ideal place to coach your child. As an alternative, laugh a lot and enjoy spending quality time with your kids. Before a competition, simply give your child a thumbs-up, a big smile, a pat on the back, or a head nod.

Love your child for who he or she is, not for the things he or she can do. Help your child have experiences in which he or she accomplishes something to feel proud about. Correct your child's misbehavior consistently and with compassion. Always give praise when it's earned. Make good eye contact with your child and give him or her your full attention when he or she is talking to show you are really listening. You are a role model, so set an example of what you value in yourself. Follow these behaviors and you will stay inside your child's Circle of Trust.

As an athlete, show appreciation to your parents for bringing you up and loving you. Look for ways to help them when you can. Say "thank you" more often. Ask your parents what behaviors of yours they like or want changed. Listen, really listen, when your parents talk to understand what they think and want. This will help you get on the same wavelength as your parents, and everyone in the family will benefit.

GRATITUDE IS NOT A PLATITUDE

The ancient Greek philosopher Plato wrote, "A grateful mind is a great mind which eventually attracts to itself great things." Several recent studies in the field of positive psychology demonstrate that expressions of gratitude can encourage individuals and groups to thrive. In fact, feeling gratitude or being thankful is one of the strengths most strongly correlated with well-being. Numerous studies have confirmed the mental health benefits of keeping a "gratitude journal" or regularly listing things for which one is grateful.

In a 2003 study published in the *Journal of Personality and Social Psychology*, Drs. Robert Emmons of the University of California, Davis, and Michael McCullough of the University of Miami demonstrated that participants keeping a gratitude journal over the 10 weeks of the study—examples of gratitude-inducing experiences listed included "the generosity of friends" and "to the Rolling Stones"—felt significantly happier, and were more optimistic about the upcoming week. They even exercised more often when compared to those instructed to record hassles (e.g., "stupid people driving") or neutral life events/social comparison.

"Find the good. It's all around you. Find it, showcase it, and you'll start believing it," said Olympic track-and-field legend Jesse Owens. Appreciation can make a real difference in an athlete's ability to feel more positive and to perform at his or her best level. Feeling gratitude sets the tone for improving and enjoying one's game and life experiences. It can also create positive relationships with family, friends, teammates, and coaches, which in turn have a positive impact on the athlete.

I encourage you to reflect on the things in your sport and life that provide you with an attitude of gratitude. This can quickly and easily be done with a gratitude journal. Recalling and writing down five good things (big or small) that happened earlier in the day or week can be an effective mood-enhancing exercise.

For example, if you remember being cheered on by a teammate during a tough practice drill, listening to a favorite song before practice, enjoying the cool breeze during a long run, or being given helpful corrections from a coach, you should take the time to write this event in your journal. This will provide you with an opportunity to briefly relive, savor, and appreciate the experience.

MEDITATION: BENCH PRESS FOR THE BRAIN

Meditation has been practiced in its various formats for thousands of years, and for good reason. For example, ancient samurai warriors used Zen meditation as an integral part of their sword training. Why? Because a quiet mind is a powerful mind. Performing with a quiet mind is a key characteristic of being in the zone. Athletes must stay focused on the task, not letting their mind wander beyond the moment, in order to play at their best level. Extraneous or jumbled thoughts (fog) reduce the quality of our focus and increase muscle tension.

Several studies have confirmed that meditation training can improve brain function and produce observable changes to the structure of the brain. Dr. Eileen Luders, an assistant professor at the UCLA Laboratory of Neuro Imaging, conducts research projects on brain morphology (form and structure) in active meditation practitioners. In a 2009 study published in the journal *NeuroImage*, Luders and her colleagues demonstrated that meditation may increase gray matter. Specifically, she compared brain scans of long-term meditators (practitioners of various meditation formats with an average of 24 years of practice) to those of people who did not meditate at all.

Importantly, meditation need not be practiced long term to have a positive physical effect on the brain. In a 2012 study published in the journal *Proceedings of the National Academy of Sciences of the United States of America*, neuroscientists Yi-Yuan Tang of Texas Tech and Michael Posner of Weill Cornell Medical College and a professor emeritus at the University of Oregon and their colleagues reported that just 11 hours of practicing integrative body-mind training, a type of mindfulness meditation, over the course of one month boosted brain connectivity and efficiency, producing positive effects on mental health.

In a 2011 issue of the journal *Psychiatry Research: Neuroimaging*, a study led by Dr. Britta Hölzel, a psychologist at Massachusetts General Hospital and Harvard Medical School, showed that practicing "mindfulness meditation" for 30 minutes a day for 8 weeks can dramatically improve the physical framework of the brain. Specifically, Hölzel and her colleagues took anatomical magnetic resonance images before and after the participants' meditation regimens and found increased gray matter in the hippocampus, an area important for learning and memory. The images also showed a reduction of gray matter in the amygdala, a region associated with anxiety and stress.

Mindfulness-based stress reduction (MBSR), a popular method of meditation introduced in the late 1970s by Dr. Jon Kabat-Zinn, was used as a therapeutic intervention in the Hölzel study. The participants were all meditation-naïve at the time they participated in the 8-week MBSR program. Specifically, the technique of mindfulness meditation uses "different objects [on which] to focus one's attention, and it could be a focus on sensations of breathing, or emotions or thoughts, or observing any type of body sensations," explained Hölzel. "But it's about bringing the mind back to the here and now, as opposed to letting the mind drift."

Mindful meditation can augment and complement all the mental skills and strategies outlined in previous chapters. Meditation is especially important for taming the reactive or emotional mind, and for sharpening concentration. Let's now conclude our discussion with a mindfulness-meditation exercise. Select a specific subject on which to focus your attention, perhaps the sensation of breathing (particularly the sound of your breath), or perhaps a verbal process like chanting a mantra or repeating a key word on each exhalation, whether "om," "one," or "calm."

Sit up straight in a chair with your feet flat on the ground or with your legs crossed on a cushion. Be present right *here* and right *now*. Close your eyes and attend to the process of breathing from moment to moment—breathing evenly and naturally and also deeply and slowly. Focus on your designated subject of attention, such as the sensation of breathing (from the feeling in your nostrils to the rising and falling of your belly). Doing so will help you keep your mind in the moment and train it from wandering around as much as the mind is prone to do.

The moment you observe that your mind has wandered from the present state—think "Hmm" (neutral/curious) instead of "Grr" (resistance/frustration). Your mind will wander in thought, such as to the past or future, and also to judgments about how well you are meditating in the moment. Simply notice when this happens and promptly return (over and over again) to the sensation of breathing. Extraneous thoughts, emotions, and sensations will rise and pass away until eventually your mind will become like still water and you will achieve a state of inner stillness. Try this exercise for 10 or 15 minutes.

Ten or more minutes of meditation practice each day can pay huge dividends. An excellent guide for developing a personal meditation practice is *Wherever You Go, There You Are: Mindfulness Meditation in Everyday Life* by Jon Kabat-Zinn, who trained the 1984 U.S. Olympic men's rowing team in mindfulness.

Make a firm commitment to practice mindfulness meditation regularly: Meditate to clear mental fog prior to your next workout or team practice; meditate to set the stage for your mental imagery or visualization rehearsal; meditate to quiet your mind the night before a competition so you can easily drift off to sleep. Indeed, to tap into the power of *now*, dedicate to meditate!

To keep moving forward, take control of your personal destiny. "It is not in the stars to hold our destiny but in ourselves," wrote William Shakespeare. Stay focused on performing daily acts of excellence in the face of temptations to get sidetracked. Look for opportunities to include others, such as joining a class at your gym or grabbing a training partner, to increase effort on simple or well-learned tasks and exercises. Talk with your family members and work together to resolve communication problems and better support each other with regard to your sports participation. Take special note of the good things in your sport and life. Launch a mindfulness-meditation practice to train your brain and develop your concentration. Always resist the pull to fall into groupthink or succumb to negative peer pressure to be less than your best.

CHAPTER SEVEN

ZEN IN THE ZONE

I'd like to
Offer something
To help you
But in the Zen School
We don't have a single thing!

—IKKYU SOJUN, JAPANESE ZEN BUDDHIST MONK AND POET

Several years ago, I had the honor of making the acquaintance of eminent martial artist Dr. Roberta Trias-Kelley. She shared several wonderful stories about her teaching practice and the life lessons she instills in her students. She explained to me that a bowl and a whip are powerful props in her karate dojo: "When I discern that a student is overthinking technique, I have them tip their head over the bowl and remind them to empty their mind. When I perceive that a student is being overly self-critical, I hand them the whip and tell them that if they are going to beat themselves up, then they should do it right!"

Former Major League Baseball all-star Shawn Green had a smooth swing and one of the most accurate outfield arms in the game. He broke or tied several records during his 15-year major-league career. On May 23, 2002, Green recorded arguably the greatest single-game hitting performance in baseball history. He was a perfect six for six at the plate (four homers, a double, a single, and a major-league record 19 total bases), leading the Los Angeles Dodgers to victory over the Milwaukee Brewers.

In his book *The Way of Baseball: Finding Stillness at 95 mph,* Green credits much of his success to learning and using Zen principles and practices. He writes,

> We believe we are our thoughts and egos and nothing more. I always suspected there was more to my true essence than my incessant and repetitive thoughts and the insatiable desires of my ego. I had been searching for that greater part of me via the exploration of Zen and meditation, but it wasn't until that meditative work took root in my swing that I truly began to disconnect my thoughts and connect with my deeper sense of being.

Zen is being fully awake without illusion in the present moment. The term *Zen* derives from the Sanskrit word *dhyana,* which means meditation or contemplation. Zen approaches to gaining wisdom can be quite effective because they are stimulating to the imagination. Zen stories provide a powerful way to bypass an overly analytical mind and instead move important information straight to the subconscious. These stories can help mobilize one's internal resources and bring them to bear on solving problems and making positive changes.

In this chapter, 22 classic Zen teaching stories and Taoist tales are presented to further deepen and expand your champion's mindset. The stories build on many of the mental skills and strategies already reviewed. Each story can impart a bit of general life help and also enhance your athletic endeavors. Each story is accompanied by a sports lesson to help connect the dots and a self-reflection question to provide you with a point for further inquiry. Make use of these principles to discover your own unique approaches and bring the lessons in at different times along your journey.

EMPTY YOUR CUP

A university professor went to visit a famous Zen master. While the master quietly served tea, the professor talked about Zen. The master poured the visitor's cup to the brim and then kept pouring. The professor watched the overflowing cup until he could no longer restrain himself. "It's overfull! No more will go in!" the professor blurted. "You are like this cup," the master replied. "How can I show you Zen unless you first empty your cup?"

Sports lesson: Always stay coachable. Taoism reminds us that the usefulness of a bowl is in its emptiness. For growth, we must be willing to leave out what we already know so we can be open to learning from others with special skills, particularly our coaches and teammates. Even the best athletes, those at the very top of their game, continually seek to learn new techniques and hone their skills. Be a really good listener and accept corrections and act on them.

Self-reflection: Am I a student of the game and open to learning?

THE MONK AND THE MIRROR

There was once a monk who would carry a mirror wherever he went. A priest noticed this one day and thought to himself, "This monk must be so preoccupied with the way he looks that he has to carry that mirror all the time. He should not worry about the way he looks on the outside. It's what's inside that counts." So the priest went up to the monk and asked, "Why do you always carry that mirror?"

thinking for sure this would prove his guilt. The monk pulled the mirror from his bag and pointed it at the priest. Then he said, "I use it in times of trouble. I look into it and it shows me the source of my problems as well as the solution to my problems."

Sports lesson: Take personal responsibility for all areas of your preparation and performance. You are responsible for maintaining a great attitude, expending your best effort during practice and in competition, and showing strong character off the field. Our background and circumstances may have influenced who we are, but we are accountable for who we become.

Regrettably, many athletes blow up at referees or competitors instead of just focusing on their own performance. To perform at a champion's level, never blame others, but focus instead on what you can do better.

Self-reflection: Do I take 100 percent responsibility for my successes and failures?

THE BURDEN

Two monks were returning to the monastery one evening. It had rained and there were puddles of water on the roadsides. At one place, a beautiful young woman was standing, unable to walk across because of a puddle of water. The elder of the two monks went up to her, lifted her, and let her down on the other side of the road, before continuing on his way to the monastery. In the evening the younger monk came to the elder monk and said, "Sir, as monks, we cannot touch a woman." The elder monk answered, "Yes, brother." Then the younger monk asked again, "But then, sir, how is it that you lifted that woman on the roadside?" The elder monk smiled at him and told him, "I left her on the other side of the road, but you are still carrying her."

Sports lesson: Play in the present tense. Always focus on winning *this* moment, not on the end result. After the game, learn to quickly let go of all downfalls and disappointments. How? Remember that everyone loses, but a champion does not dwell on his or her defeats. Give yourself credit for and celebrate what you did well, grab all of the positive corrections, and scrub from your memory everything else. This will help you lighten your load.

Notice that during interviews before key games star players will always just focus on the game at hand, almost refusing to talk about a past game or one three games away. They keep their attention on the immediate rather than looking past the upcoming game. For sports fans, it almost drives us crazy, because we want to know what they think about the playoffs and such. Maybe it's one reason why star athletes are where they are.

In baseball and golf in particular it is said that the best players have short memories. If a baseball player has a poor at-bat, strikes out, and continues to dwell on it for some time afterward, chances are he will make an error in the field or struggle in his next at-bat as well. Likewise, when a golfer is still fuming about a bad bounce or a missed putt, he or she will rarely be in the right mind-set to make a good swing on the next shot.

Self-reflection: What burdens am I still carrying from my sports experiences that I need to leave behind?

A DROP OF WATER

A Zen master named Gisan Zenkai asked a young student to bring him a pail of water to cool his bath. The student brought the water, and after cooling the bath, threw onto the ground the little that was left over. "You dunce! Why didn't you give the rest of the water to the plants? What right have you to waste even one drop of water in this temple?" The young student attained Zen in that instant. He changed his name to Tekisui, which means "a drop of water."

Sports lesson: Wring the most out of your mental and physical capabilities. Don't throw away even a single drop (of sweat) by holding yourself back. Attend to the little details in your preparation. Make the best of every situation. Rather than getting upset at having to wait for an open practice court, take the time left waiting in the parking lot to stretch or warm up. Or take what appears to be a boring training exercise and put all of your concentration into making it the best possible training exercise without waste.

An acquaintance who has helped with organization of the Ironman triathlon shared with me that he has noticed that elite athletes really don't waste anything, in their preparation or kit bag, and especially during the race transition stages where they switch from, say, swim gear to bike gear. Regarding excellence, "use it or lose it" always rings true.

Self-reflection: Do I give everything I have to give?

MAYBE

Once there was an old farmer who had worked his crops for many years. One day his horse ran away. Upon hearing the news, his neighbors came to visit. "Such bad luck," they said sympathetically. "Maybe," the farmer replied. The next morning the horse returned, bringing with it three wild horses. "How wonderful," the neighbors exclaimed. "Maybe," replied the old man. The following day, his son tried to ride one of the untamed horses, was thrown, and broke his leg. The neighbors again came to offer their sympathy on his misfortune. "Maybe," answered the farmer. The day after, military officials came to the village to draft young men into the army. Seeing that the son's leg was broken, they passed him by. The neighbors congratulated the farmer on how well things had turned out. "Maybe," said the farmer.

Sports lesson: Don't be quick to judge events as good or bad. Don't write the review until after the game or season is completed. Stay levelheaded—avoid becoming too high with the highs and too low with the lows along the way. Always make the best of the present situation regardless of what's on the scoreboard.

Self-reflection: Do I stay calm and centered when the sports gods hurl hardships my way?

CLIFFHANGER

One day while walking through the wilderness, a man stumbled upon a vicious tiger. He ran but soon came to the edge of a high cliff. Desperate to save himself, he climbed down a vine and dangled over the fatal precipice. As he hung there, two mice appeared from a hole in the cliff and began gnawing on the vine. Suddenly, he noticed on the vine a plump wild strawberry. He plucked it and popped it in his mouth. It was incredibly delicious!

Sports lesson: Seize the opportunity. Always seek the positive. The symbolism of the plump wild strawberry emphasizes that we should concentrate more on the pluses (the beauty and simple joys) than the minuses (the danger and troubles) during each moment of our lives. Have a love of the game and the competition and the particular challenge of the moment, whatever it may be.

I think one of the most exciting aspects of watching basketball is when a top player, especially a point guard, seems to be running up the court into swarming defenders, and then all of a sudden tosses up a nice alley-oop to a teammate for a slam dunk. These moments are like plucking the strawberry. Their eyes see the opportunity!

Self-reflection: Do I focus on positive achievements and existing opportunities during practices and games?

THE GIFT OF INSULTS

There once lived a great warrior. Though quite old, he still was able to defeat any challenger. His reputation extended far and wide throughout the land and many students gathered to study under him. One day an infamous young warrior arrived at the village. He was determined to be the first man to defeat the great master. Along with his strength, the old master had an uncanny ability to spot and exploit any weakness in an opponent. He would wait for his opponent to make the first move, thus revealing a weakness, and then he would strike with merciless force and lightning speed. No one had ever lasted with him in a match beyond the first move. Much against the advice of his concerned students, the old master gladly accepted the young warrior's challenge. As the two squared off for battle, the young warrior began to hurl insults at the old master. He threw dirt in his face and spat at him. For hours he verbally assaulted him with every curse and insult known to mankind. But the old warrior merely stood there, motionless and calm. Finally, the young warrior exhausted himself. Knowing he was defeated, he left feeling shamed. Somewhat disappointed that the old master did not fight the insolent youth, the students gathered around and questioned him. "How could you endure such an indignity? How did you drive him away?" "If someone comes to give you a gift and you do not receive it," the master replied, "to whom does the gift belong?"

Sports lesson: Don't let others push your buttons. Refusing to let negativity from others get in the way of your preparation and performance is how you can "own your own buttons" and keep your emotions in check. New England Patriots coach Bill Belichick is always telling his team to "ignore the noise" or disparaging and distracting things people say or write about them. On the field, ignore any "noise" coming from your opponents—don't take the bait of gamesmanship.

For example, consider eight-time world champion boxer Floyd Mayweather Jr. He is known for taunting his opponents in and out of the ring, but he himself never loses his composure. He does it to gain an advantage over opponents who let it get to them. American mixed martial artist Chael Sonnen has developed a similar approach to goading his UFC opponents.

Self-reflection: Am I strong enough not to let heckling get to me? Am I big enough to back down from trouble?

WORKING VERY HARD

A young but earnest Zen student approached his teacher and asked the Zen master, "If I work very hard and diligently, how long will it take for me to find Zen?" The master thought about this, then replied, "Ten years." The student then said, "But what if I work very, very hard and really apply myself to learn fast—how long then?" The master replied, "Well, twenty years." "But if I really, really work at it. How long then?" asked the student. "Thirty years," replied the master. "But I do not understand," said the disappointed student. "At each time that I say I will work harder, you say it will take me longer. Why do you say that?" The master answered, "When you have one eye on the goal, you have only one eye on the path."

Sports lesson: Take care of the process and the results will take care of themselves. Athletes often worry so much about where they want to end up that they lose track of the particular day-to-day things they need to focus on in order to get there. Stick to the improvement plan, one mindful step at a time, and your talent will naturally grow. Excellence does not happen overnight or in a sudden flash, and therefore it should be properly nurtured.

In the triathlon world, the elite athletes constantly warn novices about overtraining and under-recovery. Aspiring triathletes will just run harder and harder in training and will not rest properly, and they end up not making the gains they want to. The mantra is to "always stick to the training plan." Work hard, recover well.

Self-reflection: Am I just mindlessly working hard, or am I aware of what I am doing?

GREAT WAVES

Onami was a great wrestler who lived in the Meiji era. His name meant "Great Waves." Onami had a peculiar problem. He was a master in wrestling and in private could overthrow even his teachers. In public, however, he would become so bashful that even his pupils could defeat him with ease. Onami decided to approach a Zen master for help resolving his problem. A roving teacher named Hakuju had just come into town on his travels and was staying at the temple. Onami went to him with his problem. "So your name means 'Great Waves'!" said the master. "Stay tonight in this temple. Imagine that you are indeed those huge billows. You are no longer a shy wrestler. Instead, you are those powerful waves, inundating everything in your path, sweeping everything away. Do this and your worries will vanish. You will become the greatest wrestler ever known." The teacher retired for the night.

Onami sat quietly in meditation. He thought about what the

master had said. He tried imagining himself as ocean waves. Many thoughts flitted through his mind. Slowly, his mind kept going back to the waves. The hours crept by. The waves began growing higher and higher. They swept away the temple vases. By the time the sun came up, the temple had disappeared; all that remained was a vast sea, ebbing and flowing.

When the priest awoke and came to Onami, he found the wrestler still deep in meditation, a faint smile playing on his lips. The priest patted him gently. "Now nothing can defeat you. You have become those great waves." Onami went back to wrestling that same day. From then on, he never lost a contest.

Sports lesson: Build a strong and distinct mental image of your ideal performance state. Your body takes all graphic mental images as if they are real and happening at the present time. As you visualize the ideal performance state, you are actually creating it. Visualization works best when your mind is clear and your body is at ease. Regulate the breath with full inhale, full exhale. This will help you be in the proper state for visualization rehearsal. Practice the art of visualization and meditation to gain more confidence for your sport.

Self-reflection: Do I imagine my ideal performance state?

THE FROG AND THE CENTIPEDE

A frog meets a centipede and, after watching it for a while, says, "It's unbelievable! How can you walk so fast and coordinate all these legs of yours? I only have four and I still find it difficult." At this, the centipede stops, thinks about it, and finds himself unable to leave again.

Sports lesson: Okay, this isn't a Zen story, but I like it because it relates to this sports psychology maxim "Overthinking leads to underperforming." Shift from "conscious" mode to "automatic" mode during competition by trusting the skills you have developed in training. Free your mind and turn it loose rather than becoming robotic. Let go of trying to control your skills—simply allow them to happen by reading and reacting on the field of play.

Did you know that there is a collection of nervous tissue running along your backbone that is primarily responsible for maintaining balance while walking? It is almost like a reflex. If we had to consciously think about how to do it, we'd have a hard time! From motor skills to sports skills, achieving an automatic state is the ultimate goal. That's the meaning of "training the muscles to do it."

Achieving an automatic state in golf, for instance, is the ability to swing the club without consciously thinking about it. Golfers work on the mechanics of "grooving" their swing on the driving range. When the best ones are playing a round competitively, they work very hard to avoid swing thoughts (save one or two while taking their rehearsal swings). They focus their attention more on their target location in playing the shot. This is crucial because the ball is struck approximately 1 second from when the swing is started. The timing of the swing will in all likelihood be disrupted by any attempt to consciously help it (control interference). As such, good golfers allow the swing to happen by letting it go on its own.

Mastering your sports skills and knowing your game will give you the green light to go unconscious in the moment of action. Baseball Hall of Famer Ozzie Smith played shortstop for the San Diego Padres and St. Louis Cardinals from 1978 to 1996. He was nicknamed the "Wizard of Oz" and won 13 straight Gold Glove Awards for his stellar defensive play. "When I'm in my groove, there is no thinking. Everything just happens," explained Smith.

In *Zen in the Art of Archery*, author Eugen Herrigel recounts how he learned from Japanese Zen masters to let the arrow fly: by going with the flow of the moment. He writes, "In the case of archery, the hitter and the hit are no longer two opposing objects, but are one reality." Practice, practice, and more practice will eventually allow the performance to give you (flow from you), rather than you giving a performance. Use the Force; don't force the performance.

Self-reflection: If I won't trust my sports skills in competition, then why am I working so hard to practice them?

TAMING THE MIND

After winning several archery contests, a young and rather boastful champion challenged a Zen master who was renowned for his skill as an archer. The young man demonstrated remarkable technical proficiency when he hit a distant bull's-eye on his first try and then split that arrow with his second shot. "There," he said to the old man, "see if you can match that!" Undisturbed, the master did not draw his bow, but rather motioned for the young archer to follow him up a mountain. Curious about the old fellow's intentions, the champion followed him high into the mountain until they reached a deep chasm spanned by a rather flimsy and shaky log. Calmly stepping out onto the middle of the unsteady and certainly perilous bridge, the old master picked a faraway tree as a target, drew his bow, and fired a clean, direct hit. "Now it is your turn," he said as he gracefully stepped back onto the safe ground. Staring with terror into the seemingly bottomless and beckoning abyss, the young man could not force himself to step out onto the log, no less shoot at a target. "You have much skill with your bow," the master said, sensing his challenger's predicament, "but you have little skill with the mind that lets loose the shot."

Sports lesson: Great things are possible when you focus on what you want to have happen in the moment of truth, not what you are afraid might happen. The disciplined mind is what differentiates athletes with similar physical skills. The goal, and your true aim, is to perform on command when the situation most demands it.

Additionally, practicing your skills in various environments and playing against opponents with different styles can elevate your game. This requires stepping outside your comfort zone. Look for new challenges with ever-higher degrees of difficulty.

Self-reflection: Do I focus on what I want to have happen in the moment of truth?

MASTERPIECE

A master calligrapher was writing some characters onto a piece of paper. One of his especially perceptive students was watching him. When the calligrapher was finished, he asked for the student's opinion. The student immediately told him that it wasn't any good. The master tried again, and the student criticized the work again. Over and over, the calligrapher carefully redrew the same characters, and each time the student rejected it. Finally, when the student had turned his attention away to something else and wasn't watching, the master seized the opportunity to quickly dash off the characters. "There! How's that?" he asked the student. The student turned to look. "*That . . .* is a masterpiece!" he exclaimed.

Sports lesson: Allow your performance to happen more instinctively, creatively, and spontaneously. Usually this involves trying "softer" as opposed to harder. Do what's natural for you rather than trying to impress others or force a specific result. Notice how a top tennis player will just flow into the ball. In contrast, mediocre players will get in their own way by becoming tense and self-conscious.

Self-reflection: Do I play out of my mind and rely on my senses when I compete?

THE KING AND THE PEACE CONTEST

There once was a king who offered a prize to the artist who could paint the best picture of peace. Many artists tried and submitted their work. The king looked at all the pictures. There were only two he really liked, and he had to choose between them. One picture was of a calm lake, perfectly mirroring the peaceful, towering mountains all around it. Overhead was blue sky with fluffy white clouds. It was the favorite of all who saw it. Truly, they thought, it was the perfect picture of peace. The other picture had mountains, too, but these were rugged and bare. Above was an angry sky from which rain fell and in which lightning played. Down the side of one mountain tumbled a foaming waterfall. A less peaceful picture would be difficult to imagine. But when the king looked closely, he saw beside the waterfall a tiny bush growing in a crack in the rock. In the bush a mother bird had built her nest. There, in the midst of the rush of angry water, sat the mother bird on her nest in perfect peace. The king chose the second picture. "'Peace' does not mean to be in a place where there is no noise, trouble, or hard work," explained the king. "'Peace' means to be in the midst of all these things and still be calm in your heart. This is the real meaning of peace."

Sports lesson: Real peace comes from within. A state of mental calm can be maintained even in the midst of all the hoopla and distractions surrounding a big game or situation by breathing deeply and concentrating all of your energy on the purpose at hand. Nothing external can affect you internally without your permission. So maintain a winning feeling regardless of the circumstances.

Athletes who have been in the zone (a guard hitting virtually every shot in basketball, a player on a hitting streak in baseball, a running back with a huge game) say that they slowed the game down mentally and were able to see the court/ball/field and react instinctively.

Self-reflection: Do I keep cool and composed in the heat of competition?

PAINTED TIGER

A monk lived in a cave in the mountains, and he concentrated his time on meditation, knowing himself, and making a painting of a tiger on the wall of where he dwelled. It was incredibly realistic, and when it was finished, he found that he was frightened when he looked at it and couldn't stay in the cave.

Sports lesson: Look at sports participation for what it truly is rather than turning it into something that it is not. Most performance anxiety stems from our imagination running wild. Instead, think of yourself as the hunter on the field and the competition as just a painted tiger. You get to choose the pictures in your mind, so create a mental image of the current challenge that will provide you with a focused and fearless emotional reaction. Think of yourself as great waves (see page 164) instead of creating a painted tiger.

Self-reflection: Do I use my imagination to ready my focus or increase my fear?

BREATHING

After one year in a monastery, a Zen monk complained, "All I have learned about is breathing." After five years in the monastery, the monk complained, "All I have learned about is breathing." When he reached enlightenment, the elderly monk smiled and said, "Finally, I have learned about breathing."

Sports lesson: Learn and practice the finer points of deep breathing. Your breathing can become shallow when you feel stressed.

When this occurs, oxygen intake diminishes and muscle tension increases. Simply prolonging exhalation, regardless of inhalation length, promotes the relaxation response. Proper breathing helps expel the stress and tension from your system and brings you back into the present. For example, notice how a successful free throw shooter will often take a deep breath before executing the shot.

Self-reflection: Do I breathe easily and deeply throughout my day?

IT WILL PASS

A student went to his meditation teacher and said, "My meditation is horrible! I feel so distracted or my legs ache or I'm constantly falling asleep. It's just horrible!" "It will pass," the teacher said matter-of-factly. A week later, the student came back to his teacher and said, "My meditation is wonderful! I feel so aware, so peaceful, and so alive! It's just wonderful!" "It will pass," the teacher replied matter-of-factly.

Sports lesson: Everything is temporary. Nothing in sports is static. Performance slumps come and go. Playing in the zone comes and goes. All athletes experience ongoing fluctuations in their mental game and performance outcomes. Don't panic when you are in a slump; it will soon end. During a hot streak in your performance, just ride it out for as long as you can. The soreness from a hard workout will eventually go away. Everything passes.

Self-reflection: Do I roll along with the ebb and flow in my performance?

CHOP WOOD, CARRY WATER

A pupil approached a great teacher and asked what activities he should undertake in order to reach satori, or enlightenment. The old Zen master answered, "Chop wood and carry water." After 10 years of faithfully carrying out these duties, the frustrated pupil returned and told his master, "I've done as you asked. I have chopped wood and carried water for ten years, but I have still not attained enlightenment! What should I do now, O Sage One?" The master answered, "Continue to chop wood and carry water, my son." The pupil faithfully returned to his duties. Another 10 years passed. During that decade, the student matured and reached satori. He returned to see his old master wearing a simple smile on his face. "Master," he said, "I have reached satori, and now I am an enlightened being. What should I do now?" The master answered, "Continue to chop wood and carry water then, O Enlightened One." The pupil bowed deeply and retired to his wood and water.

Sports lesson: Master the fundamentals of your sports skills. High-quality training is a key to greatness in sports. "Spectacular achievements are always preceded by unspectacular preparation," observed Roger Staubach, a Hall of Fame quarterback for the Dallas Cowboys.

Be totally absorbed in whatever it is that you are training in the moment rather than spacing out or overanalyzing things. Keep it simple, because nothing extra or special is required.

Self-reflection: Am I mindful at practice or do I just go through the motions?

GOING WITH THE FLOW

An old man accidentally fell into the river rapids leading to a high and dangerous waterfall. Onlookers feared for his life. Miraculously, he came out alive and unharmed downstream at the bottom of the falls. People asked him how he managed to survive. "I accommodated myself to the water, not the water to me. Without thinking, I allowed myself to be shaped by it. Plunging into the swirl, I came out with the swirl. This is how I survived."

Sports lesson: Adapt your thoughts, feelings, and actions in response to changing circumstances, such as today's lineup, practice schedule, or field conditions. A rigid and defensive mind-set makes the situation a lot worse. Go with the flow to maintain optimal performance. You gain control by giving it up.

When the game clock is winding down, the fans are screaming, the other team has switched tactics, or the referee has just ejected your teammate from the game, don't try to find a solution—embrace the tempest and emerge victorious!

Learn to thrive in situations of pressure. Want the ball for the last shot, the opportunity to make a tournament-winning putt, or the chance to lead a game-winning touchdown drive. Many kids dream of nailing the buzzer beater to win the championships or hitting the walk-off home run to win the World Series. Don't let that edge give way to fear of failing in the moment of highest pressure.

Self-reflection: How well do I accommodate myself to unexpected or unwelcome situations?

DESTINY

During a momentous battle, a Japanese general decided to attack even though his army was greatly outnumbered. He was confident they would win, but his men were filled with doubt. On the way to the battle, they stopped at a religious shrine. After praying with the men, the general took out a coin and said, "I shall now toss this coin. If it is heads, we shall win. If tails, we shall lose. Destiny will now reveal itself." He threw the coin into the air and all watched intently as it landed. It was heads. The soldiers were so overjoyed and filled with confidence that they vigorously attacked the enemy and were victorious. After the battle, a lieutenant remarked to the general, "No one can change destiny." "Quite right," the general replied as he showed the lieutenant the coin, which had heads on both sides.

Sports lesson: You have to make your own destiny. You accomplish only what you profoundly believe you can accomplish. So believe that you are destined to achieve big things in your sport, while earning it through intelligently applied hard work. When in doubt, flip a two-headed coin! It will thus become a self-fulfilling prophecy.

Self-reflection: How great could I play if I thought and acted as if it were impossible to fail?

CHASING TWO RABBITS

A martial arts student approached his teacher with a question: "I'd like to improve my knowledge of the martial arts. In addition to learning from you, I'd like to study with another teacher in order to learn another style. What do you think of this idea?" "The hunter who chases two rabbits," answered the master, "catches neither one."

Sports lesson: This shot, this moment. The path to victory is taken one shot (or play or pitch) at a time. Bring full attention to the particular shot at hand, not getting ahead of yourself or trying to do two things at once. If you try to do everything, you will end up with nothing. The next play can wait.

Have confidence in your training program and your game plan for competition. Trust your coach and his or her input. You want to be selective about who else you ask for advice. Bring a "one-rabbit" mentality to your game. A tennis coach recently shared this story with me: "I had a mother who asked me to teach her kids tennis.

She then also took the kids to another coach. One of the kids came back to my lesson with another stroke mechanic. I knew everything was doomed from then on."

Self-reflection: Do I place all of my energy and effort on doing one good thing at a time?

THE INN

A famous spiritual teacher came to the front door of the king's palace. None of the guards tried to stop him as he entered and made his way to where the king himself was sitting on his throne. "What do you want?" asked the king, immediately recognizing the visitor. "I would like a place to sleep in this inn," replied the teacher. "But this is not an inn," said the king, "it is my palace." "May I ask who owned this palace before you?" "My father. He is dead." "And who owned it before him?" "My grandfather. He too is dead." "And this place where people live for a short time and then move on, did I hear you say that it is not an inn?"

Sports lesson: A sport will always outlive us. It's all borrowed time. Every competitive sports career must inevitably come to an end at some point. And, like many record holders have said, "Every record is meant to be broken." The sports team we play on is like the inn from the story—we are just passing through.

Gary Mack, a former counselor for the Seattle Mariners and the Phoenix Suns, said, "Success comes from the peace of mind of knowing you did your very best on and off the field as a player and as a person. When you leave the game, how do you want to be remembered?" Make the most of the time you do have so that when you leave the game there are no regrets.

Self-reflection: When I leave the game, how do I want to be remembered?

THE STATUE

A young man had a clay statue, a family heirloom. He'd always wished that it were bright shiny gold instead of plain brown clay. When he began to earn a living, he put aside a little now and then until he had enough for his special project: to have his statue covered with gold. Now it looked just the way he wanted it to, and people admired it. He felt very proud that he had a gold statue. However, the gold plating didn't stick to the clay very well, and it wasn't long before it began to flake off in spots. So he had it gold-plated again.

Soon he found himself using all his time and resources to maintain the gold facade of his statue. One day his grandfather returned from a journey of many years. The young man wanted to show him how he had made the clay statue into a gold one. However, clay was showing through in many spots, so he was somewhat embarrassed. The old man smiled and held the statue lovingly. With a moist cloth he gently rubbed it and gradually dissolved some of the clay. "Many years ago, the statue must have fallen in the mud and become covered with it. As a very young child, you wouldn't have known the difference. You forgot, and thought it was just a clay statue. But look here." He showed his grandson the place where the clay was removed, and a bright yellow color shone through. "Underneath the covering of clay, your statue has been solid gold from the very beginning. You never needed to put more gold on to cover the clay. Now that you know what its nature really is, all you have to do is gently remove the clay and you'll reveal the gold statue you've possessed all along."

Sports lesson: The key to peak performance lies within you. Remember, if you can spot the greatness in others, then you already have some of that greatness in yourself. See the gold in the mud and celebrate the gold. Remove the mud by eliminating doubts and other mental interference—let your gold shine through. You have an inner greatness waiting to be unleashed. Tap into your total potential.

Self-reflection: Do I see myself as a champion?

As we've learned from tales like "The Burden" and "Taming the Mind," Zen stories can teach us much about how to perform at a champion's level. Are you like the humble monk who takes personal responsibility for his situation in "The Monk and the Mirror"? During stressful situations, are you like the peaceful bird under a raging waterfall in "The King and the Peace Contest"? Make sure to ask yourself and think about the self-reflection questions. The Zen stories are keyed in on the enduring challenges that humanity has faced for eons, so remember to incorporate a few lessons into your sports training.

CHAPTER EIGHT

GOLDEN
REFLECTIONS

It is one thing to study war and another to live the warrior's life.
—TELAMON OF ARCADIA, MERCENARY
OF THE FIFTH CENTURY B.C.

This chapter starts with a Zen proverb:

> To follow the path,
> look to the master,
> follow the master,
> walk with the master,
> see through the master,
> become the master.

The Olympic Games are the biggest and most watched sporting event in the world. The Olympic medal structure—gold, silver, and bronze—provides the athlete, the press, and those that watch this event with a tangible record of great personal and team success for each top participant in the Summer and Winter Games. In the following pages, we will see inside the minds of athletes who turned obstacles into stepping-stones and won one or more Olympic gold medals to reach the pinnacle of their sport.

"Gold medals aren't really made of gold. They're made of sweat, determination, and a hard-to-find alloy called guts," said Dan Gable, one of the most renowned wrestlers—and wrestling coaches—ever. Gable won a gold medal at the 1972 Olympics in Munich. Not a single point was scored against him in six matches. As the University of Iowa's wrestling coach, Gable compiled a record of 355–21–5, and his team won 15 NCAA championships.

Keep in mind that winning an "inner" gold medal is your ultimate victory. A true champion is someone who has overcome great odds to reach the pinnacle of his or her potential, regardless of the externally measured result. Each mental master provides an exclusive glimpse into a personal journey into the champion's mind-set. They all won on a world stage, some by bouncing back from serious injuries, while others were triumphant against all odds in their quest for gold. Everyone can learn a great deal from the lessons these champions share—lessons forged in the Olympic crucible. So learn the champion's mind-set and take the gold medal advice from some of the world's greatest athletes, including:

- **DUNCAN ARMSTRONG,** an Australian swimmer who won gold at the 1988 Seoul Olympics.

- **JON MONTGOMERY,** a Canadian skeleton racer who won gold at the 2010 Vancouver Olympics.

- **GABRIELE CIPOLLONE,** an East German rower who won gold at the 1976 Montreal Olympics and the 1980 Moscow Olympics.

- **ADAM KREEK,** a Canadian rower who won gold at the 2008 Beijing Olympics.

- **DANA HEE,** an American martial artist in tae kwon do who won gold at the 1988 Seoul Olympics.

- **NICK HYSONG,** an American pole-vaulter who won gold at the 2000 Sydney Olympics.

- **PHIL MAHRE,** an American alpine skier who won gold at the 1984 Sarajevo Olympics.

- **NATALIE COOK,** an Australian beach volleyball player who won gold at the 2000 Sydney Olympics.

- **GLENROY GILBERT,** a Canadian sprinter who won gold at the 1996 Atlanta Olympics.

AUSTRALIAN
DUNCAN ARMSTRONG,
OLYMPIC GOLD MEDALIST IN SWIMMING

CAREER HIGHLIGHTS

- 1988 Seoul Olympics gold medalist (200-meter freestyle)
- 1988 Seoul Olympics silver medalist (400-meter freestyle)
- 1986 Edinburgh Commonwealth Games gold medalist (200-meter freestyle)
- 1986 Edinburgh Commonwealth Games gold medalist (400-meter freestyle)
- 1989 NCAA all-American in the 400-meter and 800-meter freestyle for the University of Florida
- Two-time Olympian (1988, 1992)

The Olympic Games have inspired men and women throughout history. Many have loved the adventure of traveling to a foreign land to compete in the games and the long-lasting memories. Others have reveled in the team atmosphere following their selection and then in living in the Olympic Village once the games began. If you're a student of the games' history, you'd be delighted by the many ways that the athletes have experienced them.

I love stories, both hearing and telling them. The Olympics are steeped in stories of courage, endurance, opportunism, and the unexpected. Herein are the stories that fueled my desire to be an Olympian from a very early age. When I was just 6 years old, I watched 16-year-old Queenslander Steve Holland win a bronze medal in the 1976 Montreal Games in the men's 1500-meter freestyle. My entire school crammed into the library to watch him have a go at winning a gold medal. I can still remember the excitement and anticipation of watching this wunderkind of a world champion represent us in our biggest gold medal chance of those games. But that day Steve was outfoxed by two better swimmers, yet he still won a bronze medal. My experience in that school library inspired me to pursue swimming as the way to go to the Olympics.

That's what makes the Olympics so hard to win; the athletes devote all those years of passion and dreaming to take part. When you get to the Olympics and represent your country, you're not just facing athletes who have prepared for the past 12 months, 2 years, 4 years, or even 10 years. You're facing highly motivated, very talented, uncompromising, and deadly serious people who have dreamed and prepared for this particular event their whole lives! You can forget what the program says at the games, because when the starter's gun goes off, anything can happen. This is why the games are such a sport-lovers' paradise. The script is being written before your very eyes and you don't know what's going to happen next.

My personal beliefs about the games prepared me in 1988 to be ready to win the 200 freestyle in Seoul. At that time, I wasn't interested in the culture of South Korea or who was on my team or what the Olympic Village was like or the number of freebies from the sponsors. At 20, after 5 years of grueling training with my coach Laurie Lawrence, I noticed all of those things, but none of them counted for anything. My unbelievable focus on what it was going to take to win was the edge I had over my opposition.

We arrived in Seoul 10 days before my race and I barely left my room: eat, train, sleep, and try not to go crazy in anticipation of the 4-year clock counting down to only a few moments in the pool. You see, athletes have just 4 years to be as ready as they can be before the gun goes off for their events at the games. You can't arrive at the games with excuses because excuses don't count when the 4-year clock stops, the gun goes off, and you have 1 minute 47 seconds to prove you are the best 200 freestyler in history. If you have an excuse in mind in this scenario, then you lose—plain and simple. You can train the house down for years and be in your best shape, and then a virus or a cold can take the edge off of you just before the games. You arrive at the starting line or block less than your best and lacking confidence—and then your opposition tears you apart. Four years of your life as an athlete goes down the drain. It sounds horrible, but it happens at every games to many gold medal hopefuls. You have 4 years like every other Olympian, and if you don't make the most of it, you can't win.

So, once I arrived at the village, I didn't go anywhere outside the village and seldom left my room for 10 days.

In 1988, I was ready, mentally tough, and confident, and only a few people knew my training times were off the chart and put me in contention for a gold medal. I had done everything I could to arrive at this race opportunity, and I just had to execute on that day against the fastest men in the history of the 200 freestyle. Easy, right?

Everything that happened over the 2 days of racing for gold in the 200 freestyle felt like it was meant to happen. Looking back on it 25 years later I'm still surprised it was so smooth. The way I competed in swimming was all about confidence through preparation. The harder I worked in training, the better I swam, although I'm sure I overtrained during a large part of my swimming career. But for those Seoul Games, my training in the years leading up to 1988 was just incredible, so my confidence came with the knowledge that I'd outtrained everyone in that race. I knew the seven other blokes in that final didn't do the training I'd handled. So when the gun went off I just had to show everyone what I was feeling inside. With this confidence, I was able to swim the first 100 meters faster than ever, knowing I had the legs to get back in the second half of the race in great form.

I did exactly this and the opposition couldn't handle my second 100 meters. I went on to break the world record and win gold.

I loved all the old stories of gold medal winners at the games, but the stories that truly inspired me were about people from humble backgrounds who went "animal" in their training for years. Then with great courage and determination, they overcame all their opposition to claim a surprising victory. I dreamed of becoming an Olympic gold medalist like Emil Zátopek, Vladimir Salnikov, Lasse Virén, and Herb Elliott—tough men who didn't compromise their training for anything and attained the ultimate prize.

CANADIAN
JON
MONTGOMERY,
OLYMPIC GOLD MEDALIST IN SKELETON

CAREER HIGHLIGHTS

- 2010 Vancouver Olympics gold medalist
- 2008 Altenberg World Championships silver medalist
- 2008 Altenberg World Championships silver medalist (mixed team)
- 2011 Königssee World Championships bronze medalist (mixed team)

Sports are a lot of things to a lot of people. They are a way out for some, a way in for others, a means to a better life for a few, and a means to an end for many. I am one of the many in the latter group, and I never would have had the courage or the confidence to discover my sport, my means to an end, and now my passion had I not believed in myself enough to try new things and live life outside my comfort zone.

Growing up in rural Manitoba, Canada, I had the great fortune to be born around the same time, in the same small town, as 16 other boys who would grow up to become amazing athletes. My friends and I grew up playing together at recess, road hockey after school, ice hockey all winter, and baseball all summer. With some of the best coaching in the province, no tryouts, and no pickups from other towns, my team from a community of 1,600 amassed a total of eight provincial championships in hockey, a Western Canadian bronze, and two provincial championships in baseball. We were always the smallest team, but we played like we were twice our size, and we never once stepped on the ice or the field without believing that we would win. I think the single greatest advantage we carried with us was our quiet confidence.

Teams that would normally intimidate others into submission were flabbergasted and completely taken aback by the way we never backed down and continued to press until the last second counted off on the scoreboard or the final out was recorded. This never-say-die attitude and belief that we would prevail in the face of great odds proved to be the deciding factor in countless competitions in which we were outmatched in nearly every aspect except one . . . our self-efficacy! Simply put, it was the belief that we would achieve that which we sought.

What I learned growing up shaped my life in adulthood. After moving to Calgary, Alberta, upon finishing my university studies, I was desperately seeking something that I could call my own and something that I could sink my teeth into. Hockey had been that "something" growing up, but since graduating from high school, I had not played competitively and craved the sense of camaraderie and self-satisfaction I got when I left everything I had on the ice. Academics filled that void to a point while I was in school, but writing tests are not the same as testing my mettle against others in athletics. It was that feeling, that physical challenge, and my lifelong dream to wear the maple leaf on my chest while representing my country at something—at anything—that inspired me to try new sports, primarily those offered only in cities with an Olympic legacy, in a search of my means to an end.

Speed skating was the first new sport I tried after arriving in Calgary in the fall of 2001. Having spent nearly my entire life on skates, I thought making the transition to speed skating would be a no-brainer. To say I was mistaken would be an understatement. The extra-thin, extra-long skate blade with no ankle support on the boot is to a hockey skate what a wooden clog is to a Jimmy Choo (my wife said that's a fancy ladies' shoe)! I really enjoyed learning to speed skate and did manage to get my mind wrapped around the difference between a hockey stride and a speed skater's stride, but I wanted to try some other sports before I settled on the one I would dedicate my efforts to mastering. Becoming a national team athlete was still my goal, and I needed to make sure I worked not only hard but also smart.

I had considered trying luge, another sport that only cities that have hosted Winter Olympic Games can offer to their residents, but after seeing a skeleton race for the first time in March 2002 on a random visit to the Canada Olympic Park in Calgary with my parents, I knew immediately that I had just seen something that I needed to try.

One month after the skeleton was reintroduced as a full-medal Olympic sport, after a 54-year absence, I was on my first run down the subzero chute, headfirst, on a sled that I later described to my friends as a cafeteria tray with rails, sliding at more than 45 miles per hour. Eight short years later, I was sliding down the mountainside in Whistler, British Columbia, during the 2010 Olympics, going nearly twice as fast while realizing my ultimate dream: wearing the maple leaf on my chest and an Olympic gold medal around my neck.

After that first run, I had no idea what had happened, but I knew without any doubt that I had found my new "something." I didn't have any idea what I would accomplish in this sport that only a week earlier I didn't even know existed, but I knew that I was going to give everything I had to find out. I believed that the only way I could find out was going to be through hard work, sacrifice, and good old blood, sweat, and tears. I really believed that this was going to be my path for success. Not a path for winning races necessarily, as I did not have control over how good I would be compared to other skeleton athletes, but I knew I could become the best slider that I could be with that winning formula. That's all I wanted to find out. How good can I be? How can I be the best *me* possible? What that leads to is not up to us. That's out of our control. What we can control is our attitude and our belief that we can achieve our personal best. Sometimes our personal best is better than everyone else's. The difference between those who realize their dreams and their own potential and those who don't starts with the belief that they can actually achieve that which they seek.

EAST GERMAN
GABRIELE CIPOLLONE,
OLYMPIC GOLD MEDALIST IN ROWING

CAREER HIGHLIGHTS

- 1980 Moscow Olympics gold medalist (women's eight)
- 1976 Montreal Olympics gold medalist (women's four)
- 1977 Amsterdam World Championships first place (women's eight)
- 1978 New Zealand World Championships second place (women's eight)

My rowing journey was a bit rocky, and when I started, nobody said I would be an Olympic champion.

I had no idea what the sport of rowing was when a recruiting coach invited me to come to the boathouse in 1970. But what I had physically and mentally was very helpful during my journey. I was tall, strong, and energetic, and I had the willpower and ambition. Up to this point, though, I participated in all different kinds of sports.

My first 5 years were not very successful and I trained because I had fun. At this time I didn't dream of being on the national team because it just seemed too far away.

My road seemed to split and I had to make a big decision in December 1975. Our club focused on preparing boats to qualify for the national team. I was so far behind that my coach wanted me to quit. Luckily, the sweep rowers (using one oar) were looking for a strong woman to row in the four with the coxswain. I was 18 years old and had to decide to give it another try or just go on to university and study to become a civil engineer.

I don't take it well when somebody tells me, "You cannot do this." My ambition really grabbed me and I was thinking, "I'll show you." I was working very hard on my technique to fit in with that crew. We qualified as a four for the Olympic team in May 1976.

I'm thankful to that coach today because his decision forced me to think about what I really wanted to do: Was I willing to use my capacities and work harder and harder to become a world-class rower or was what I had accomplished up to that point enough for me. Both ways are fine, I just needed to decide which way to go and do it with 100 percent commitment.

My women's eight carrier went to the 1980 Olympics with a lot of lessons to learn. Having seen our race in Moscow not long ago, I remember every part of it very clearly.

Our coach's strategy focused on the Soviets as our toughest competition. We knew their last 250 meters (out of the 1000-meter race) would be their slowest. Our goal was to stay close to them and not let them get more than half a boat length ahead of us at 250 meters to the finish line.

The reality looked surprisingly a bit different to us. Our coxswain shouted at us that the Soviets were more than a boat length ahead with only 250 meters to go.

I remember thinking that this situation cannot be true; we have to do something very quickly. It seemed like everybody in the boat had the same thought, and the boat took off. We had enough room to catch the Soviets with our last two strokes.

All eight of us adjusted to the new situation, listened to our coxswain, and worked even harder as a team to reach our goal. There was a very fine line between being overtaken by negative thoughts (i.e., giving up and losing) and positive thinking (i.e., telling ourselves to go for it and hopefully win).

The whole team showed a great spirit, and I'm very grateful to them.

Now as a coach, I'm teaching my athletes that it is okay to have a weak moment in practice or in a race. We are all human. The important thing is not to give up, to know it can happen, and to trust that you can pick it up again and be even stronger than before. That moment has to be practiced again and again.

I believe mental strength in a race can be the decision maker between winning and losing at any level.

CANADIAN
ADAM
KREEK,
OLYMPIC GOLD MEDALIST IN ROWING

CAREER HIGHLIGHTS
- 2008 Beijing Olympics gold medalist (men's eight)
- 2007 Munich World Championships gold medalist (men's eight)

- 2003 Milan World Championships gold medalist
  (men's eight)
- 2002 Seville World Championships gold medalist
  (men's eight)
- Two-time Olympian (2004, 2008)
- 2010 Canadian Athlete Leader of the Year
- 2005 Stanford University Athlete of the Year

The best advice I ever received was a question from Mike Spracklen, my Olympic coach: "Do you want to win, Adam? Do you?" It was not just the question, but the timing of the question. He would ask this question when my actions did not align with my goals. I would hear this when I was late for practice, not recovering properly, performing poorly, or being lazy.

We need mentors in our life who can be honest and challenge us with powerful questions. These questions drill into our core and uncover the deeper motivation we need for world-class success. When statements questioning our motivation are asked at the right time, we access a higher spiritual and psychological drive.

I believe that the conscious presence in each moment is the golden key to effective practice. Practice is not about going through the motions with our body while our mind and spirit reside elsewhere. Rather, practice is about focused effort with our entire being. This engrains habit and skill into our unconscious self. The goal of being in the now during practice is to create an unconscious competence within our mind, body, and spirit.

A great tool I use for bringing back presence is to imagine a teacher, a coach, or a monk standing over my shoulder. When I start thinking about or connecting with anything other than the task at hand, my guide shouts at me, "*Be here now!*" Then I get back to the task at hand with my full being.

The obvious goal of athletic competition is to win. However, I find that focusing too hard on attaining the win weakens our ability to perform. It is comparable to finding the perfect man or woman, or filling your bank account with cash. If you only focus on the result, you stay single and poor. Instead, we must focus on the higher goal: uncovering our authentic, best self.

Competition exposes the core of our emotional, spiritual, and psychological being. Rivals act as an extreme, external motivation that helps us go deeper to find our best and worst qualities. In competition and challenge, we find our inner truth. How hard are you willing to work on competition day? How skilled are you? How well did you prepare for the day? What stops you from displaying your best self? What does it feel like when your best self shows up?

Be mindful of your reactions during, before, and after competition, but do not judge them. Observe your behaviors and take note. Noting your reactions to outside inputs will give you the important questions needed for improvement. Then ask your coach, sports psychologist, or spiritual mentor. Exploring these questions will give you more strength for practice, your next competition, and life after sport.

If you search for your authentic, best self during competition, you will find it. Victory often comes along for the ride as a pleasurable side effect.

Initially, I expected the Olympics to be bigger than life and my nerves to be supersize. Instead, the games were surprisingly close to normal. They felt like just other races. Initially, my familiarity and comfort felt weird; then it scared me. To cope, I needed to remove judgment of my reaction and trust that my body has a wisdom that is greater than the intelligence of my analytical brain.

A ritual that I have developed throughout my competitive career helped me keep my sanity the day of my Olympic race. This is a ritual that helps me get to the right level of nerves. Having no nerves is bad.

You need nerves to perform at your best, but when nerves fuel negative thoughts and fear, nerves are also bad.

The day of any big race, competition, or test I continually tell myself, "Today is a very special day—a day like any other day, but a little more special. Today is Race Day!" Race days, and specifically my Olympic race day, were just that: special. By labeling our competition days as "special" we can take unexpected psychological reactions in stride. The unexpected reaction is expected on special days.

There are many arrows in the quiver of an effective team. However, there is one arrow that is always missing from teams that fail: buy-in. All team members must fully commit their spirits to the goals of the team.

Time after time, I've seen overconfidence and personal pride destroy the potential of a team. Your ideas are valuable only if they are good enough to be adopted by your coach and teammates. If your opinions are rejected, let them go.

A mantra all teams should adopt is "If you wanna win, you gotta buy in." This is an active choice and it can be difficult. Buying in makes you vulnerable, and it requires that you diminish your ego. You lose some control. You need to let go of ideas from previous teams and outsiders.

The athlete must say to him or herself, "I choose to commit a hundred percent to the philosophy, goals, and outcome of my team. I commit to my role on this team." This means listening to and trusting your coach as well as your teammates. You must distance yourself from the opinions of people outside your team. The media, parents, friends, and armchair quarterbacks all have opinions that can disrupt your buy-in.

If your team has strong buy-in, your quiver will have a sharp and true arrow to shoot.

AMERICAN
DANA
HEE,
OLYMPIC GOLD MEDALIST IN TAE KWON DO

CAREER HIGHLIGHTS

- 1988 Seoul Olympics gold medalist (women's lightweight division)
- 1988 United States National Championships silver medalist
- 1987 Barcelona World Championships fifth place
- 1987 United States National Championships silver medalist
- 1986 Berkeley World University Games bronze medalist

The difference between a great athlete and a gold medalist is all in the frame of mind. If you can believe it, you can achieve it. I know this for a fact. As an Olympic gold medalist in the full-contact fighting sport of tae kwon do, I have found this to be true time and time again.

Yet considering that I was abandoned and abused since the age of 3, raised in an orphanage, and lived on the streets at age 15, how did I learn this? Especially since by the time I was a young adult, I had learned to run from any chance, challenge, or dream because I had very little self-esteem or self-confidence. In fact, I was my own worst enemy of success. So then, how did I do it? How did I make this 180-degree turnaround?

One step at a time!

First came the desire, the dream. Next came the determination. Then I learned the importance of focus, perseverance, and preparation. And finally, all of these things taught me to believe in myself.

Nothing will ever change without movement. Even if it is the wrong step to take, a single action can open doors that you would not believe. It can give you insight that you never would've thought you had. Never be afraid to take a chance and take one small step.

Do not focus on the whole end result of what you want. Focus only on each tiny step you take forward, and each step will lead you to another step. Imagine crossing a river that is shallow but very fast and dangerous. If you look at the far shore, seeing the power of the water, the risk, you may turn right on around. However, look around the bank and find a single stepping-stone. Put that first stone in the water close to the shore. Then, using that first stone, place another stone, and so on. Before you know it, you will reach the other side just by keeping your focus on each little thing you need to do right then. You have no room for your fears to derail you. We often think our goal is insurmountable, when in fact it is only one step away.

There is only one truth about perseverance and that is this: Perseverance happens when failure is not an option. Never give up, no matter how hard your task. And if you hit a roadblock you cannot seem to overcome, figure out a way around it. Me? I was badly injured going into the Olympic Games. My back injury could not be helped, and I could not train. If I could not train during those final weeks, I stood no chance of winning. Well, I did train—in my mind. I used visualization to practice the movements, the timing—everything. By the time my competition came around, my back was rested enough to allow me to compete, and my mind made up for what I lacked physically.

Preparation is the shell that holds the egg together. Without preparation you just have one sticky gooey mess. Entering the Olympic stadium on competition day, I felt good. Warming up, I felt ready. My mind was convinced that this was *my day*. Only, something happened right before I entered the arena that blew my psyche. All of a sudden, my old fears rushed into my mind and I lost my self-confidence. Yet I had sacrificed so much to be here. I knew I had the speed, the strength, and the training. I knew that I had done everything possible to be prepared for this exact moment. That's when it hit me: "Hey, I *am* ready. I *am* good enough!"And I shoved those doubts aside and took that final step into the competition ring. Olympic gold! Yet, if I had known that I had not been fully prepared, I know I would have crumbled.

For the first 25 years of my life, I ran from any chance, challenge, or dream, and I felt like a failure. Now, after the Olympics, more than 17 years as a top stuntwoman, and as a top motivational speaker, I have learned that even when I lose, I win. For nothing can ever take away that feeling deep inside of pride and satisfaction for having the courage to do what I wanted to do regardless of fear, obstacles, or setbacks.

Great things are possible—with just one step at a time.

AMERICAN
NICK
HYSONG,
OLYMPIC GOLD MEDALIST IN POLE VAULT

CAREER HIGHPOINTS

- 2000 Sydney Olympics gold medalist (ending a 32-year Olympic gold medal drought for the United States in the pole vault)
- 2001 Edmonton World Championships bronze medalist
- 1994 NCAA champion for Arizona State University
- Two-time Pac-10 champion (1993, 1994) for Arizona State University
- 1990 Arizona state high school champion

I've had to deal with quite a few injuries over my career. I have learned that many of my injuries gave me good opportunities to focus. Making rehab your new sport is a great way to think. Furthermore, I think injuries give you definitive evidence of a weakness you have and force you to focus on that weakness Many ankle and knee injuries occur because of poor stability, and treating these injuries should make you address that weakness, perhaps making you stronger in the end.

In 1998, I had an ankle surgery that put me in a cast for 8 weeks during my season. I used that time not only to excel at my rehab but also to work on the swinging part of my pole vault. I practiced on a high bar daily. During my first competition after the injury, I jumped 18' 8" easily, and over the next 8 years the constancy level of my vaulting improved by nearly a foot. I went from averaging 18' in a competition to averaging 18' 8" to 18' 10". I also won an Olympic gold medal and a World Championships bronze medal. Many of my injuries were blessings in disguise; this one certainly was.

I tell my athletes to think of things this way: Working to improve at your sport or to reach a goal is like climbing a mountain. Mountains have gradual inclines, steep inclines, and cliffs, and these paths don't always lead to the summit. Sometimes the path heads down or drops before it starts rising again. These declines in the mountain's path are akin to injuries, illness, or other setbacks in training. As long as we as athletes keep following and moving forward on the path, we are doing what is necessary to be the best we can be. It is easy when things are going uphill because you can see yourself getting closer to the summit, but you have to stay focused on the goal when the path heads down.

Simply worrying and feeling sorry for yourself won't move you forward on the path; don't just focus on the fact that you went downhill. Yes, you should be concerned that you went downhill, as concern indicates that you acknowledge that the path isn't quite what you wanted or hoped for, but you should also be inspired by that concern and address the problem with a new goal of moving forward on the path. If you are sick and can't practice, you can choose to get depressed because of your problem, which would most likely prolong your recovery period, or you can do what it takes to get better faster: rest, drink fluids, see a doctor, and eat right. By excelling at rehab, you will move forward on the path.

AMERICAN
PHIL
MAHRE,
OLYMPIC GOLD MEDALIST IN ALPINE SKIING

CAREER HIGHLIGHTS
- 1984 Sarajevo Olympics gold medalist (slalom)
- 1980 Lake Placid Olympics silver medalist (slalom)
- 1980 Lake Placid World Championships gold medalist (combined)

As 10-year-olds, my twin brother, Steve, and I watched Jean-Claude Killy of France win three gold medals in the 1968 Olympic Winter Games in Grenoble, France. Everyone made a huge deal of this feat, and it was then that the two of us began dreaming of representing our country in the 1976 Olympic Games in Innsbruck, Austria.

Five years later, in the spring of 1973, I was named to the U.S. ski team and everything seemed to be on track to make my dream a reality. But the best-laid plans don't always go smoothly. The following November, days before I was to go to Europe for my first international competition, I was caught in an avalanche and broke my right leg. Missing the 1974 ski season would make my dream difficult, but my focus never wavered from making the 1976 Olympic team.

Unfortunately, the good Lord had other plans. Maybe he felt I wasn't mentally strong enough yet and needed more time to gain mental strength, as I refractured my leg 9 months later and missed most of the 1975 season as well. I would only have the months of December and January 1976 to compete in international competitions to qualify for the games in February. With great determination and focus, my results were good enough to earn a spot on the team, and I went on to finish fifth in the giant slalom.

That result set the wheels in motion for a new goal: 1980 Lake Placid, New York. With the same determination and focus for the next three seasons, I was very successful and won races and became a true contender each and every time I left the starting gate. But once again the best-laid plans were interrupted when I fractured my left ankle in March 1979, just 11 months prior to the games. This injury required a 4½-hour surgery to put seven screws and a 2-inch steel plate in my ankle to hold everything in place. I had been down this road before, so I never gave up on my goal of competing in the games. Although I was physically not fully recovered, mental strength enabled me to compete and win a silver medal in slalom. The questions then were "Do I plan another 4-year journey?" and "Will I be healthy or competitive?" The answer to both was "Why not!"

In 1984, in Sarajevo, Yugoslavia, I would have my last chance for Olympic gold. At this time in my career, I knew all too well just how difficult medals were to win, let alone a gold medal. Everything must be in place—health, physical strength, and most important, mental strength and focus. This was the first Olympics I competed in without having to deal with an injury beforehand. Two solids runs, one mistake-free, would be enough for victory.

I look back on my career with fond memories of the competitions, the wins and losses, but most important, the journey. It is a journey that teaches you all of life's lessons through sports. Dream, and dream big!

AUSTRALIAN
NATALIE
COOK,
OLYMPIC GOLD MEDALIST
IN BEACH VOLLEYBALL

CAREER HIGHLIGHTS

- 2000 Sydney Olympics gold medalist
- 1996 Atlanta Olympics bronze medalist
- 2003 Rio de Janeiro World Championships bronze medalist
- Five-time Olympian (1996, 2000, 2004, 2008, 2012)

From an early age, I was encouraged by my grandfather to dream big, to say, "That's what I want," and then go about getting it. That is what I did at age 8. I said I want to win an Olympic gold medal. I didn't know how or in which sport, but I was inspired by a fellow Aussie who won a 1982 Commonwealth Games gold medal.

Once you've set a "that seems impossible" goal, don't just put it in an envelope or on your dream chart where no one else can see it because you're afraid that if you don't make it you'll be seen as a failure. My philosophy is once you have decided what it is you want, then tell as many people as you can with conviction. I told people 2 years before the games that I was a Sydney 2000 Olympic gold medalist. Once you tell people with that much conviction, not only do you now have to walk, talk, and act like a gold medalist (all the time), but people can then start to support you in all sorts of ways you didn't even think possible.

Of course, there will be naysayers who say you can't do that, and they may even laugh at you. You just need to ignore them, move on, and maybe even decide not to hang around those people again. You have to cut some people loose whether they're friends, family, or co-workers if they're not supportive. Otherwise, it will be extra weight to carry on the journey.

In the beginning, I was afraid to tell people I was going to win gold, and I had some of my fellow athletes telling me I was an idiot and asking why I was saying that and telling me it was embarrassing. I just surrendered, and every day it got stronger in me and my whole life began to become engulfed in gold—I had a gold toaster, gold sunglasses, gold watch, gold car, Palmolive Gold soap, gold sheets, gold boxer shorts—everything was gold. Every time I saw something gold, it acted like a magnet, drawing me close toward it. It was sending a very powerful message to my subconscious mind: There was no option for me other than gold.

People often ask me what if I had come in second, and I comment by saying I would have painted the silver medal gold. See, it is not about the medal. It is about living a gold medal life. The final test is during that one day at the largest sporting event on earth, and the medal is a symbol rewarding you for your efforts. But I was rewarded every day along the path. The whole journey was golden. What are you going to start doing today to make your life *golden*?

All of this is easy when things are going great, but it's when life isn't going so great—when you're at the bottom of the pile—that you need to know your strategy to get yourself back on top. Often it's about support; you need to surround yourself with a team of people and you need to ask for help. There's this belief out there that it's weak to ask for help, but it's not. We call it *teaming*; when you team up with someone, it takes the pressure off and gives you someone to support and be supported by. We can all find someone to hold hands with through life, whether it's our partners, coworkers, or an organization teaming up with other organizations. This way, the world would be much better off.

CANADIAN
GLENROY GILBERT,
OLYMPIC GOLD MEDALIST IN TRACK AND FIELD*

CAREER HIGHLIGHTS

- 1996 Atlanta Olympics gold medalist (4x100-meter relay)
- 1997 Athens World Championships gold medalist (4x100-meter relay)
- 1995 Pan American Games gold medalist (100 meters)
- 1995 Göteborg World Championships gold medalist (4x100-meter relay)
- 1993 Stuttgart World Championships bronze medalist (4x100-meter relay)
- Participant in eight Olympic Games—five as an athlete (1988, 1992, 1994, 1996, 2000) and three as a coach
- 2004 Olympic Hall of Fame inductee
- 2008 Canadian Sports Hall of Fame inductee

I see sports as a metaphor for life. The lessons I've learned as an athlete have translated into my everyday experiences, and I believe they've made me a better, more selfless person. I had to learn discipline and perseverance, but I also learned how to be a great teammate and how to appreciate the steps along the way, rather than focusing only on the end goal. Those lessons have been invaluable to me—as an athlete and as a human being.

What first drew me to sports was the competitiveness. I loved the

---

* This exclusive interview with Glenroy Gilbert was conducted for *The Champion's Mind* by Amanda Sage, the founder of Kickass Canadians (www.kickasscanadians.ca).

idea of testing myself against another person. But once I got serious about track and field, it didn't take me long to realize there are always people who are more talented than you, and if you try to compete against them, you'll be disappointed. So I started setting goals I could personally attain, or try to attain, rather than concentrating on who I was trying to beat. It was almost like an evolution from competing against folks to understanding that I had to start to see what I was capable of based on my own talents.

That's not to say that talent is the most important thing. If I were to use percentages to examine what it took for me to succeed, I would say it's probably 70 percent hard work and 30 percent talent. I never really saw myself as overly talented; I just saw myself as someone who didn't know when to stop. I put it all out there every single time. I would definitely say it was more hard work than talent, in my case.

I don't think there's any real recipe for success. It involves all the things that most people think about when they consider what it takes for an athlete to reach the podium: hard work, dedication, and perseverance. It's all of that. But I think the number one factor is luck.

I took a lot of chances throughout my career. When I competed in bobsled in the 1994 Lillehammer Winter Olympic Games, anything could have happened on the hill. We crashed a bunch of times. I took training for track and field seriously, but I didn't mind taking chances along the way, and I was lucky they worked out for me.

The primary reason I started bobsledding was that I was exhausted from the narrow focus of track and field. I was getting frustrated and stale in the sport, and I wasn't seeing the gains that I thought I should. So I decided to bobsled because I thought if I spent a winter pushing a bobsled, I'd essentially be making myself stronger and fitter for the acceleration phase of the 100-meter sprint—the first 40 to 50 meters.

As it turned out, that's exactly what happened. The very next summer I ran my personal best in the 100 meters, and it all came off the heels of bobsledding. I'd taken a risk, and many people thought I

wouldn't be able to come back to form in track after spending a season bobsledding. But breaking up the monotony of track and field
helped me—physically and mentally. When I returned to sprinting, I
felt a renewed energy and focus, and I think that was a big factor in
why I was able to sustain such a long career.

I continued to try different things now and then, so I'd always have a
sharp focus when I returned to track. For example, I accepted an invitation to try out for the San Francisco 49ers in the spring of 1996—although
that was cut short when I split my hand open while receiving a pass.

Regardless of the outcome, finding ways to stay hungry and
focused was extremely beneficial for my athletic career. I draw on
that lesson now, as a coach, by encouraging my athletes to take the
time to recover—not just physically but also mentally. That can be hard
when you're dealing with young athletes who want to push hard all
the time. But it's important that they see the big picture when they
consider their athletic goals. Even when your event is the 100 meters,
your career is always going to be a marathon, not a sprint. You have
to be able to enjoy the process.

I don't deny that winning gold at the 1996 Atlanta Summer Olympic Games was a highlight of my career. But I see that run as a com-
ing-of-age moment—for me as an individual and for the entire relay
team. Our journey culminated in the Olympic gold medal, but it
began in 1992 and involved a prolonged transformation that took
place over a period of about 4 years. We had a lot of great runs and
a lot of disappointments along the way. But we persevered through it
all, and that's what led us to winning gold in Atlanta.

Yes, we won at the Olympics, and that's what every athlete strives
for. But it wouldn't have been possible if we hadn't gone through
everything that came before. That's one of the biggest lessons I've
taken from my career: It's not just about one moment, it's about a long
series of moments that add up to something much bigger than any
individual victory.

In this chapter, we've learned from several athletes about their mental approach to achieving greatness. These champions have much they can teach us about how to perform at a champion's level, in sports and elsewhere in our lives, with the same intensity as an Olympic athlete. Take some time right now to think about each of these gold reflections. How is what these gold medalists went through similar to what you're going through now? What can you learn from the decisions these champions made?

Where are you on your journey from good to gold medal? Are you going to emulate Duncan Armstrong by keeping your eyes on the prize? Will you stay positive and persistent while recovering from injuries until you get your game back like Nick Hysong and Phil Mahre? When you are going through tough times, are you going to stay tough-minded like Dana Hee? All of us can learn to think, feel, and act like a champion, so remember to incorporate a few lessons from these Olympic gold medalists into your own game.

CHAPTER NINE

YOUR WORLD-CLASS
GAME PLAN

By failing to prepare, you are preparing to fail.
—BENJAMIN FRANKLIN

How can you pull together all of the information you need to produce one easy workable plan? The key to this, and to one's primary objective, is to establish a mental plan of attack that lets you move forward. Begin by measuring the mental state of your game with the mental game scorecard provided. This will help you develop a winning mental practice and competition plan. Next, create your own pre-performance readiness routine so that you are at full power when the gun goes off or when the puck is dropped. Learn how to give yourself a winning pregame pep talk when needed, and make sure to keep an eye out for the mental errors athletes make at major events. And strive to find emotional balance in life's continuous imbalance, ambiguity, and uncertainty by controlling what you can control.

MENTAL GAME SCORECARD

In what areas of the mental game do you do extremely well? What comes less naturally? First, rate your current mental game performance to identify your strengths and target areas for growth. Second, think through what you need to do and thus are going to do to develop your mental skills and strategies to their highest level. Third, decide precisely how you are going to make use of your mental skills and strategies both in practice and in competition. Fourth, establish your personal mental game plan and solidify its thinking in your mind so you'll be ready to use it when you need it.

Here is a working mental game scorecard you can use to quickly measure the mental state of your game. Take a few minutes right now to review your performance in training and competition for the previous 3 months. Rate your current mental abilities from 1 to 10 (1 = low, 10 = high) honestly and accurately for the following mental skills:

___**GOAL SETTING:** I have clear daily improvement goals and I know exactly what I want to accomplish in the long term.

___**MENTAL IMAGERY:** I vividly see and feel myself performing well.

___**SELF-TALK:** I keep my thoughts simple, positive, and powerful.

___**CONFIDENCE:** I have a can-do attitude when I need it the most.

___**FOCUS:** I stay on target and in the moment.

___**BREATH CONTROL:** I breathe easily and deeply under pressure.

___**MENTAL TOUGHNESS:** I do what is hard and stay positive under adversity.

___**ANXIETY MANAGEMENT:** My butterflies fly in formation.

___**ENJOYMENT:** I incorporate fun, play, and humor into my game and avoid becoming serious, dull, and uptight.

___**BODY LANGUAGE:** I carry myself as a champion.

___**INTENSITY:** My energy level stays just right for the situation (not too up, not too down).

___**PERSONAL AFFIRMATIONS:** I regularly repeat my power phrases with meaning and conviction.

MENTAL GAME SCORE: ___

How well did you score? The total score for the personal assessment can range from 12 to 120, with the average score around 60. Build your mental game so your total score is at least 84, equal to a 7 or more for each item. Subsequently, strive to sharpen each skill even further. Do keep in mind that these mental skills are interconnected, so working on one area of your mental game will strengthen other areas, too.

Your mental practice plan. Here is an example of how your mental game improvement plan might look: Imagine that you scored lowest on "Confidence." You then set a goal to emphasize that skill for, say, 21 days. Reread "Confidence: Flex Your Confidence Muscle" (see page 40) and review the seven questions for flexing your confidence muscle. Pledge to maintain confident body language and facial expressions as you practice. Identify a past peak performance and relive it in your mind's eye.

Resolve to always be in the process of improving. That way you'll also be developing one or two of your mental skills during the day for a set number of days. You might do it for 7 days or for 21, but whatever goal you set, stick to it. Importantly, this practice does not have to be time intensive. For example, you can practice breath control (15-second breaths) when you're stopped at a red light, waiting in line, or during any brief downtime during your day. A "Go for the gold!" sticky note or dot can be a helpful prompt.

Your mental performance plan. Think of game day as showtime, not time for practice. Sam Snead, a Southern gentleman and one of golf's great champions, liked to say, "Dance with the one you brung." In competition, this means you have to go with what you've got and it's not time to be switching things around. Make whatever adjustments are necessary, but don't try to fix your game while you play it. Don't let what you don't have get in the way of what you do have. Recognize and maximize what is in you today. Stay in it to win it by focusing on what is working well in the present.

In terms of your mental game, set two or three goals for each competition. Identify specific keys to stay in a winning frame of mind for the entire contest. Write down these mental goals, or ABCs, on an index card and take it with you to the competition. These goals should be worded positively and in the present tense so you can focus on what you want to have happen, not on what you hope to avoid (e.g., write, "Stay on target" not "Don't get distracted").

In selecting your mental goals for competition, determine the specific areas of your mental game that are most important for you to underscore in your game play at this particular time. Do you need to breathe deeply to keep physical tension to a minimum? Are you maintaining positive body language no matter how the competition is unfolding? Do you refocus quickly when distracted or after making a mistake?

The ultimate experience is to go out there and battle to the absolute best of your abilities; actualizing your mental game goals will help bring out your best in today's contest. Modify your mental game goals for each competition and decide what is most important to accentuate at that particular time and place.

Here is a sample mental game plan you can use for competition:

My goal today is to battle to the best of my abilities. I will accomplish this goal by following my own ABCs:

A. I play with purpose and passion.

B. I'm on a one-good-play-in-a-row mission.

C. I think, feel, and act confidently all the way through that mission.

PREGAME MENTAL PREP

Baseball legend Hank Aaron said, "The most important thing is how a guy prepares himself to do battle." A pre-performance routine is a prescribed, detailed course of action to be followed regularly on game days so that you are mentally and physically ready to battle right when the action starts (rather than firing too soon or too late). Having a simple and dependable routine gives you a head start on your competitors. Routines provide reassurance and predictability that can help to alleviate PCS, or Pre-Competition Syndrome—the added nervousness, excitement, and irritability most athletes experience prior to performing.

A really good routine helps to marry mind and body to operate as one unit on the field. A routine also provides a shield from all types of distractions, such as unsolicited advice from others or mind games (talking smack, etc.) from an opponent trying to psych you out. Simply ignore any such irrelevancies during pregame. For example, some athletes take refuge in their headphones by listening to their favorite music, whereas others close their eyes and visualize themselves executing their game plan.

How do you get ready to play ball? Here's some mental homework that can help you further develop your own pregame strategy. Reflect on how you thought, felt, and prepared prior to your best and worst games. What were the similarities and differences in your approach during these times? These contrasting performance outcomes are not coincidental or random events, but were influenced by what you did before competition. Maybe ask your teammates and coaches for their feedback as well.

What do you do before a game to set the right tone? Self-awareness is the key to change.

- Do you listen to your favorite song(s)?

- Do you spend a few minutes visualizing optimum performance?

- Do you practice slow, deep breathing to quiet your mind and steady your body?

- Do you like to be social with your teammates, or do you stay in your own world?

- Do you avoid interacting with negative people to stay in a good mood?

Look for patterns in your mental and physical pregame tendencies to transform any poor patterns into top-notch patterns. What helps you to excel? What causes you to fall short? What makes it easier to avoid distractions? Do you let the importance of the match affect the way you prep beforehand? Also, reflect on mid- and end-game patterns (e.g., Are you solid midmatch or do you experience a breakdown? Are you able to seal the deal to win the game?).

After identifying your tendencies, formulate a plan of attack consisting of what you need to do mentally in order to peak your performance. Having a working routine will help you get to the starting line with the ideal mind and mood. Sticking to your routine from one competition to the next will allow you to compete more steadily and reliably throughout the season.

In building your readiness routine, especially for the hour or so before game time, determine how to activate your thoughts and emotions in order to fully tap your physical talents. Make sure to review your mental game goal list the day before, and spend a couple minutes going over it during pregame. Going through the same physical warmup routine that you typically do in practice can also help take your mind away from worrisome thoughts and help you avoid nit-picking your technical skills. Remember to focus on what is going well that day.

Do what is best to perform at your best. A collegiate gymnast shared with me her recent discovery that dancing around and socializing with her teammates at meets helps her perform at a higher level, in comparison to her previous custom of trying to spend quiet time by herself. Russian Fedor Emelianenko, a retired mixed martial arts heavyweight who during his prime went undefeated for nearly a decade, enjoyed relaxing and playing a few games of cards with his training team in the locker room before his fights.

Unfortunately, some athletes abandon their routine when it is most needed. Develop the discipline to stick to your routine before each and every competition regardless of the importance of the game or your particular opponent. However, be prepared to adjust your routine accordingly in case there is a delay in the start time or you arrive later to the venue than expected. Make modifications when one component of your routine becomes stale or if you find something that better suits your needs. Give it a test run before a practice or training session to evaluate its effectiveness.

Canadian Duff Gibson, the gold medalist in the skeleton at the 2006 Turin Winter Olympics, shared with me his mental readiness approach. He explained,

> When I competed, my prerace routine was something that I had fine-tuned over many years, but at the same time I was always ready to modify it to better suit my physical and mental state and/or the environmental

conditions. For me it was important not to be too regi-
mented because I didn't want a change in schedule or
some unforeseen circumstance to have the ability to
throw me off my game. Typically I didn't listen to music.
I preferred quiet because I felt it allowed me to be more
self-aware with respect to the progress of my warmup.
I needed to be in tune with my energy levels so that I
could achieve that balance in which my muscles and
nervous system were primed but not taxed. I also needed
to be aware of any muscular tightness or other physical
issue that either I or our team therapist would need to
address.

What do you typically do postgame? Important things to do
after a competition include stretching, eating recovery foods,
drinking adequate fluids, and appreciating and talking with others
about what worked well in the game. Think about the positives.
Wait until later in the evening or the day after to complete your
game analysis in your Champion Journal or to reflect on what you
could have done better.

Do not get carried away by superstition. Most athletes have developed
superstitions or embrace lucky artifacts such as coins, bracelets, or
articles of clothing. Our beliefs about these personal artifacts can
help us center ourselves and thus provide a great distraction from
performance anxiety. Along with a good routine, artifacts can keep
your good wolf a winner by serving as a positive prompt.

American gymnast Danell Leyva was the 2011 U.S. national
gymnastics championships all-around gold medalist and went on to
win the bronze medal in the all-around at the 2012 London Olympics. He is known for the "lucky towel" he has incorporated into his
routine during competition. Like a tennis player between sets,
Leyva drapes the towel over his head to keep out distractions.

Luckily for his fellow competitors, he keeps the towel clean. Leyva jokes, "I do wash it. It's not all sweaty and nasty."

At the same time, though, you should avoid becoming so carried away with props or rituals that they become distracting. If this happens, it could be due to anxiety run amok, and you will need to directly address the underlying causes of worry and stress. Superstitions and the like are of course not necessary to delivering great performances. New York Yankee great Babe Ruth, dubbed the "Sultan of Swat" for his prowess at the plate, shared his stance on the topic of superstitions: "I only have one superstition. I make sure to touch all the bases when I hit a home run."

PERSONAL PEP TALK

A quick pep talk to yourself can often help get your mind geared up before performing on the day of competition, especially when the Big Bad Wolf of doubt begins to howl. Pep talks should be tailored to your particular needs and competition conditions. Here are five keys to an effective pregame personal pep talk.

1. Keep it simple, clear, and *powerful*.

2. Evoke previous success for *confidence*.

3. Tell yourself what you need to *focus* on to play your best.

4. Remember that there is nothing to lose and everything to *win*.

5. Make a decision to *enjoy* each moment.

Let's listen in on two winning pregame speeches from college basketball during March Madness. Notice how the five keys are covered in both of these speeches. It is vital for a coach to know what makes his or her team tick. Otherwise, there's a chance you will inadvertently psych your team *out* instead of *up*. The first speech, by University of Florida coach Billy Donovan, was delivered before their NCAA championship game in 2006 against UCLA. The Gators ended up winning the game against the Bruins, which was the first of their back-to-back NCAA championships. Here's Coach Donovan:

> Guys, tonight is not about the past and it's not about the future. It's about right now. You guys have got to want this night to last forever. You've got to want to run and play and defend, all night long. You've got to live in the moment, and understand there's going to be adversity, and there's going to be challenges. That is what has brought us close together as a team, the adversity and the challenges. Live in the moment, cherish each moment, and go out there and play as a team.

The second speech is by University of Kansas coach Bill Self. It was delivered before the NCAA championship game in 2008 against the University of Memphis in which the Jayhawks pulled off an upset victory over the favored Tigers. Here's Coach Self:

> You guys have had an unbelievable year; the winningest team in Kansas basketball history. Think about that. You are the winningest team in Kansas basketball history. Nobody can ever take that from you. Nobody. So if they can't take that from you, basically we got nothing to lose tonight. Nothing. But we got so much to gain. The reason I feel so confident about us winning is because we don't have to change one bit who we are. For thirty-nine games, you displayed how hard you're going to play, you displayed how you're going to guard, you displayed how you're going to rebound, and you displayed how we're going to steal extra possessions. All we have to do is be ourselves. Let's go have some fun.

Now imagine for a second that you are a competitive swimmer; you sit in the ready room right before your race at a dual meet against your main rivals. As you notice the other top swimmers present, the Big Bad Wolf of doubt begins to howl. How do you counter the Big Bad Wolf? Here's a sample pep talk you could give yourself by using process or task-relevant thoughts:

> Okay, let's take a few deep breaths to clear my mind and get centered. I'm well prepared and ready to race. The other swimmers have to beat me; I don't have to beat them. Over and over again, I've visualized my hand touching the wall first. It's time now to focus on what I will do to swim fast and get today's best performance. I'm going to trust my stroke mechanics, nail my turns, and charge home on the finish stretch. I have nothing to lose but everything to gain. I'm going to cherish each moment as it comes. I'm bringing everything I've got, so let's free it up, go have some fun, and make a big splash!

MENTAL ERRORS AT MAJOR EVENTS

Don't lose the game before you play it.

—DARRELL ROYAL, FORMER HEAD FOOTBALL COACH AT THE UNIVERSITY OF TEXAS

Let's draw attention to the three big mental errors (MEs) athletes often make at major events or on the day of the big game, such as a playoff or championship contest. The big MEs are 1) overemphasizing the outcome, 2) trying too much, and 3) tracking the negative. Making these MEs leads to preventable performance slipups on the field. To perform at a champion's level, you can win the game from within by putting a stop to these errors. Fortunately on those days, there are mental corrections (MCs) to those errors that you can perform. Regardless of what stage of the season, the particular opponent, or the game's significance, the top goal is always the same—to compete at your best from start to finish. Upon doing so, you will have achieved your best total performance on that day.

Here's what Nick Saban, head football coach at the University of Alabama, asked his team before the 2012 BCS National Championship Game: "How bad do you want to finish? What's your effort going to be, your enthusiasm, your excitement to play in the game, the toughness you're willing to play with, all the intangibles, and will you do it one play at a time?" The Crimson Tide went on to dominate the LSU Tigers 21–0 for the win. Alabama focused on playing one play at a time versus overemphasizing the outcome. They did what they were coached to do rather than doing too much. They followed the positive track instead of tracking the negative. Pay attention to what Saban shared postgame with reporters:

> We certainly didn't play a perfect game. We got a field goal blocked. We couldn't score a touchdown for a long time. But the guys just kept playing and never once was anybody ever discouraged about anything that ever happened in the game. And I think that attitude prevailed for us as a team. We were just going to play one play at a time, finish each play. And regardless of what the circumstance was on the play before, have a sort of . . . "I will not be denied" attitude about how to play the next play. And I think that spirit was sort of reflected out there in the way our players competed.

Mental Error 1: Overemphasizing the outcome. Peak performance is available only in the present moment, so deciding to overemphasize the outcome of the big game is a costly ME and one frequently made by athletes. Why? It is because of all the preparation that has already been put into the effort, along with having such high hopes for winning (or reaching best times) or fear of losing (or failing to reach best times). Making this ME by thinking too far in advance about the possible consequences of victory or defeat often leads to playing well below one's ability because your focus becomes diluted. Minimize the magnitude of the big game beforehand. Don't think about hoisting the trophy, think about playing the game.

If you are prone to overemphasizing the outcome when the spotlight is on, the MC you need to make is to *stop stressing yourself out about winning or losing.* If you focus on the process, the score will take care of itself. Execute your game or race plan step-by-step, thinking only of the next step to take. As soon as you notice you have wandered off to thoughts of what is going on beyond your team or worrying about the final outcome, make the MC. Promptly redirect your focus back on your mission of mastering the here and now, making sure you are concentrating on doing your job. Work the process and keep it happening one good play (or shot or lap) at a time until the final whistle or you've crossed the finish line. The outcome can wait.

Do not allow your mind to be used up or your physical energy to be wasted on external factors over which you have no direct control. This includes any irrelevancies related to the competition or the hoopla of the event. Remain centered on the purpose at hand from start to finish by attending to the little details or performance keys that are always within your personal control. This process orientation is particularly important when you are fatigued or the game clock is winding down. Don't chase the win, let the win find you.

Mental Error 2: Trying too much. This is also a common ME made by athletes during a championship game, when playing on the national stage, or when going against a higher-ranked opponent. It is because they arrive overeager to play due to the anticipation and expectation that naturally surrounds that contest, as well as mistakenly believing that they need to play better than their previous best. Rather than trying too hard and becoming tense and reckless as a result, simply play consistently through the whole game. There is a false belief that you must make a Herculean effort or have a superhuman performance because of the circumstances. However, making this ME will deplete your energy and only move you away from what's made you successful in the first place.

The MC you need to make is to *stick to what you know has made you successful,* including following your regular routine on the day of competition. You deserve to be here in this situation. If you are well prepared, you do not need to change anything else right before or during the game that you haven't already worked on in prior practice. Do your normal excellent job and battle to the best of your abilities—nothing else is needed. Trust the talent you have from training and be instinctive with your decision making and automatic with your physical skills.

Mental Error 3: Tracking the negative. Demanding perfection in your performance (or insisting on ideal conditions) every time out is another frequent ME made by world-class athletes. This is especially prevalent in major international events such as the Olympic Games, Wimbledon, or World Cup. Many competitors do not stop and realize there is always some margin for error. There is a frequent misconception that every play, shot, or possession by you or your teammates must be perfect in order to win (or that your self-worth is at stake). However, making this ME will only move you from being up to becoming uptight.

The MC you need to make is to *follow the positive track* instead of tracking the negative. Put an immediate stop to a negative or Big Bad Wolf commentary running in your head after something unexpected or unwanted happens. This might be a turnover made by your team or a call missed by the officials. Refuse to get sucked into frustration, panic, or pessimism. Immediately leave the blunder behind (i.e., flush the mistake) or you will drag it into the next play or possession.

Always make a commitment prior to performing that you will do your best to take whatever happens out there in stride. Emotionally rebound and let go of the negative events or mishaps that will happen in the course of events on the day of competition. This champion attitude will help you stay cool and confident for the whole game and allow your talent to carry you forward.

FOUR-FOOT PUTTS AND PARALLEL UNIVERSES

Let your soul stand cool and composed
before a million universes.

—WALT WHITMAN

Sports psychologist Bob Rotella authored the bestselling book *Golf Is Not a Game of Perfect*. Golf is certainly not a game of perfect, and strange things happen, like a ball getting stuck in a tree. The hole is 4.25 inches in diameter and the standard U.S. ball is 1.68 inches in diameter, so every time the ball is over the hole, it falls in—unless gravity fails, which it won't.

Why, then, do most golfers dread a 4-foot putt? Because of their mind-set, most notably when their thoughts are clouded by doubt. Great putters, however, differ from others in their mind-set: The great ones see the ball going in before they attempt the putt. Sure, they'll miss a few, but they'll make many more. The point is to see what you imagine and you'll have a better chance of realizing what you saw.

Imagine the following scenario on a Sunday at a future U.S. Open. Our hero, Jack, is playing golf at the exact same time in three parallel universes. In each universe, he is on the 18th green and faced with the same 4-foot putt. If he sinks the putt, he wins his first tournament.

- In the Bronze universe, he is too excited.
- In the Silver universe, he is overly worried.
- In the Gold universe, he is calm and focused.

In the Bronze universe, Jack believes that making this putt will transform his life. His mind fills with images of the spoils of victory. He is overexcited because he is anticipating victory rather than staying in the moment. Jack rushes through his preputt routine. He tightens his grip, stabs at the ball, and runs it 3 feet past the cup—a crushing outcome.

In the Silver universe, Jack believes that missing the putt will ruin his life. His mind fills with images of disgrace and ridicule. He is trying not to miss rather than living in the now and being in it to win it. After dawdling during his preputt routine, and while nervously looking around, he tightens his grip, stabs at the ball, and leaves it a foot short—an embarrassment.

In the Gold universe, Jack thinks, "Read it, roll it, hole it." He looks at the gold dot on his golf glove and takes a deep breath. He's not worrying about making the putt, only how he makes it. All he is thinking about is starting the ball on the right line with the right speed. In this narrowly focused moment, Jack's only thought is *execution*. That is, he is concentrating on what he can do physically rather than the meaning of a make or miss. He loosens his grip, makes a fluid stroke, and hears the ball drop into the cup—a thrill.

Remember that thoughts determine feelings, and feelings influence performance. Jack's physical skills were the lone constant in all three universes. The made putt in the Gold universe reflects his right frame of mind, without the mental static about the meaning of the putt that disrupted the Bronze and Silver universes. His mind was clear (fogless) and his body was calm, totally centered on the task.

Jack accepted that making this putt would add to his life, not determine it—his self-worth and future happiness were not on the line. He was not troubled by what others would think about his made or missed putt. With that champion's mind-set, he followed his preputt routine and performed with total trust and freedom.

Always focus on the process and execution rather than worrying about the desired, or worse, the feared result, whether you are staring down a putt on the 18th green to win a tournament or to break 80 for the first time. To be more like Gold Jack, apply what you've learned here; otherwise, you don't know Jack!

BEND, DON'T BREAK

Like the bamboo tree, bend but don't break.

—ANONYMOUS

Do your best to strike a balance between your sport and life. However, all of the talk in the media about achieving a total "life balance" can be misleading because *everything* is constantly changing. The expectation that balance or perfection (or a manageable workload) is simultaneously possible in all areas of your life is a misperception.

While one part of your game is on an upswing, another part may be on a downswing. Perhaps you are doing well in your sport, but you aren't spending time with your friends. Sometimes you feel 100 percent, and other times you feel ill. Occasionally you play well and your team still loses a close game.

There are also periods when a particular part of your life becomes all-consuming out of necessity, such as during training camp for football, preparing for final exams, or during playoff time in your sport. Demanding a total sport-life balance at these times is idealistic.

Instead, stay centered by aspiring to find the emotional or inner balance in life's continuous imbalance, ambiguity, and uncertainty by flowing with changes and controlling what you can. The celebrated 16th-century French essayist Michel de Montaigne remarked, "Not being able to govern events, I govern myself." Sometimes life deals you a very difficult hand. To perform at a champion's level, play the hand you're dealt the best you can—because that is all you can do.

The champion's mind-set is your ace in the hole. Learn it and use it. Ask yourself the following two questions:

1. How will I handle my current situation like a champion?

2. What will I do now to get to where I want to be in the future?

As previously discussed, stop sweating the stuff you cannot control. Instead, govern yourself and control the controllable by adhering to these reminders:

- In regards to whatever is weighing on your mind right now, realize that this too shall pass.

- Focus your energy on problem solving in the present rather than excessive worrying about the future.

- Take positive-action steps instead of succumbing to apathy and inactivity.

- Be assertive by supporting your rights and needs, such as taking the necessary time for your training and regeneration. Sometimes this requires placing concern with your interests above the interests of others. That is, learn when to say no to others and hold to it in order to reduce stress or stick to your priorities.

- Talk with friends and family or a specialist for help and support rather than becoming or staying isolated.

- Continue to be brilliant with self-care basics and relaxation techniques for tension release.

- Maintain a boundless sense of humor—find the funny side or silver lining in your situation.

- Above all, take a goal-line stand in protecting the core values related to your long-term health, happiness, and close relationships in the process of achieving success. As a thriving client of mine expressed, "Always keep your sanity over success."

Begin your well-trained disciplined action right here and right now to make solid and lasting changes in your mental game. You are fully equipped with the knowledge to build and implement a mental plan of attack that lets you move forward in the direction of your dream goals. Knowing this, are you going to continuously hone each one of your mental skills? Are you going to make mental corrections when it matters most? When it comes to working hard and intelligently on your mental game, don't just talk about it, be about it!

CHAPTER TEN

LONG-TERM SURVIVAL OF THE MOST MENTALLY FIT

*The toughest thing about success is
that you've got to keep on being a success.*

—IRVING BERLIN

A ttaining and sustaining success in sports always comes down to a survival of those most mentally fit. A strong commitment to excellence in training intensity and time over the long haul is required to progress as an athlete and to achieve your personal best. If you want to succeed and to move through difficult times, it is crucial to make an ongoing commitment to achieving superiority in your sport through the daily practice of cultivating a champion body *and* mind.

Excellence is not random. It is also more than a short-term ambition, accident, or accomplishment. It is developed by design and achieved by setting and tenaciously pursuing high, competitive goals. The greatest champions in history have all had a long-range vision and plan of what they wanted to accomplish in tandem with a complete daily devotion to their specialization. Having daily or weekly improvement goals to meet will help ensure that you are always working right.

Are you like a chicken or a pig? The fable of the chicken and the pig exemplifies the difference between involvement and commitment. In the fable, a chicken is talking to a pig about opening up a breakfast eatery. The chicken says, "Let's name the restaurant Ham-N-Eggs!" The pig ponders all that he would be risking and says, "No, thanks. I'd be committed to the breakfast, but you'd only be involved."

To perform at a champion's level, think of your sports career as the restaurant proposal from the fable. The pig realizes that giving yourself completely to a process (high commitment) increases the possibility of success. In other words, go all-in on the labor necessary to become the best possible athlete. Don't be a chicken that wants to be only half involved in the process (low commitment). Unless you fully invest in your sports career, you will be selling out on achieving your dream goals.

Pat Riley is a former coach and player in the NBA. Currently he is team president of the Miami Heat. Riley has won an extraordinary nine NBA championship rings—four as Los Angeles Lakers head coach, two as Heat president, one as Heat head coach, one as Lakers assistant coach, and one as a player for the Lakers. According to Riley, "There are only two options regarding commitment. You're either in or you're out. There's no such thing as life in between."

Sustained obsession. Brad Alan Lewis and his rowing partner Paul Enquist won the gold medal in the double sculls at the 1984 Los Angeles Olympic Games, becoming the first U.S. rowers to capture gold since 1964 and the first U.S. doubles team to secure gold since 1932. For Lewis, high commitment equals sustained obsession. He explains how he went from good to gold medal in his book *Wanted: Rowing Coach:* "If anyone here is secretly dreaming of making the Olympics, I can tell you exactly how to do it, two words:

Sustained Obsession. The obsession isn't so hard. But keeping it sustained is a tough nut to crack."

I was intrigued by Brad's personal approach to excellence, so I asked him to share more about how he thought and what made him tick. His response:

> In regards to sustaining obsession, it helps to be obsessive going in—certainly that's pretty much the case with me. I have always had an obsessive nature. Neither my brother nor my sister are similarly cursed. Along the same lines, I cannot multitask at all—so that I can easily devote 100 percent of my energy to winning a gold medal, but not 83 percent. Can't do it. So naturally everything else in your life suffers, for years on end, but that's the way it goes. I was able to sustain my obsession by breaking my training life down into 1-day segments. Pretty much each day I would do battle against my training opponents, of which I had many here in Newport Harbor [California]. These opponents deserve most of my medal since I could not have pushed myself to necessary levels of pain without them alongside.

Setting golden priorities. How important is it to reach best times or achieve your sports or fitness dream goals? Whether it is running a sub-3:10 Boston-qualifying marathon, playing your sport in college, or contending in the Olympics, this is a critical question to ask yourself. The higher your sports or fitness goals, the more you will need to emphasize thinking and doing the right things to achieve those goals. This requires a genuine determination to endlessly improve in all key areas of your performance, covering all aspects of your mind-set, nutrition, exercise, relationships, and regeneration.

"We talking about practice, man. I mean how silly is that?" Remember those infamous words from Allen Iverson? Well, sports legends and gym rats from Walter Payton to Larry Bird to Tiger Woods prioritized high-quality training and continuous improvement above all else. One athlete shared with me that hearing about Michael Jordan always going to the courts early to shoot free throws for an hour provides inspiration to do the necessary grunt work in his own game. Here's Dan Gable, one of the all-time greatest wrestlers/coaches, on the importance of setting priorities, especially regarding practice:

> When you finally decide how successful you really want to be, you've got to set priorities. Then, each and every day, you've got to take care of the top ones. The lower ones may fall behind, but you can't let the top ones slip. You don't forget about the lower ones, though, because they can add up to hurt you. Just take care of the top ones first. In 25 years as a head coach and assistant, I think I might have missed one practice. Why? Because practice is my top priority. A day doesn't go by when I don't accomplish something in my family life or my profession, because those two things are my top priorities.

Priorities will need to be adjusted in the off-season and will be different than during the season. Your priorities may also evolve throughout your playing career. For example, consider 15-time NBA all-star Kobe Bryant. He has in recent years shared with the media how he is increasingly prioritizing nutrition to stay on top of his game. Specifically, he eats more lean meats and vegetables, while slashing some of the favorite junk foods that he enjoyed eating earlier in his career. "It sucks, but it's worth it," Bryant said about watching his diet.

Do what others won't do. Soccer star Lionel Messi, who plays for La Liga club FC Barcelona and serves as the captain of the Argentinean national team, won the 2011 FIFA world player of the year award, thus becoming the first player to win it three times in a row. Messi was golden again in the 2012 season, breaking German Gerd Müller's 40-year-old record for most goals in a calendar year and finishing with a remarkable 91 goals. For his accomplishments, he was crowned as the world's best for a record fourth time.

Messi is all-in with his commitment to individual and team greatness. He explained, "I made sacrifices by leaving Argentina, leaving my family to start a new life. . . . Everything I did, I did for football, to achieve my dream. That's why I didn't go out partying, or a lot of other things." The superstar forward has been willing to make the necessary sacrifices as part of his dedication to reaching his total potential as a player and as a teammate.

Jerry Rice was known as one of American football's most motivated and hardest workers during his Hall of Fame career. His rigorous personal off-season training routine put him in tip-top shape for training camp each year so he was able to dominate the competition and stave off injuries. His workouts included sprinting $2\frac{1}{2}$ miles up steep hills. Multitudes of NFL players came to train with him over the course of his long career, but most wouldn't stick around very long.

Rice declared, "Today I will do what others won't, so tomorrow I can accomplish what others can't." He maintained success at the highest level by working hard and intelligently while doing everything that was required. He dedicated his life to the pursuit of greatness while staying in love with his sport. He also wasn't afraid to surround himself in training with other top players and was thus able to better develop his abilities.

Resilience and appreciation. Bob Tewksbury is a former Major League Baseball pitcher originally from Concord, New Hampshire. He was drafted by the New York Yankees out of Saint Leo University in the 19th round of the 1981 draft, and although he suffered through a string of shoulder and arm problems throughout his career, he pitched solidly in the big leagues for over a decade. He had his best season in 1992 with the St. Louis Cardinals, finishing with a 16–5 record while posting a 2.16 ERA. Notably, he played in the all-star game and was third in Cy Young Award voting that year.

As a former player and now a mental-skills coach for the Boston Red Sox, Tewksbury is in a special position to talk about the topic of developing and maintaining a pattern of success in athletics. Prior to the start of MLB spring training in 2013, he shared his experiences and insights about this topic. Two general themes emerged from our discussion about his baseball accomplishments: resilience and appreciation. He said:

> I overcame two arm surgeries, [after] the second of which the doctor performing the surgery didn't think I would ever pitch again because of the injury. I was traded, released, and was sent down six times from the major leagues to the minors. Due to the injuries and demotions I had an appreciation for the game that not all players have. I understood how being a major-league player for a day was a gift, let alone eleven years.

So, what does Tewksbury believe are the primary reasons why some baseball players that have the physical tools fail to maintain success? While acknowledging that this is a difficult question, and noting that there are several likely explanations, Tewksbury right away identified a couple of primary reasons. First, there can be a "loss of motivation based on early success and financial reward." Second, some players show an unwillingness or inability "to adjust with age to continue to perform at the major-league level."

Tewksbury provided some examples of athletes making changes over time: "A pitcher having to adjust his style of pitching from a power pitcher to a control-finesse type; a hitter changing his approach at the plate from long ball power to more the other way, with an up-the-middle approach."

Refresh and recharge. Be completely committed, but at the same time, be careful not to overextend yourself. That is, you have to be strategic about your choices and be assertive about regeneration to avoid burnout. Swiss tennis star Roger Federer has won a record 17 Grand Slam tournaments and has completed the career Grand Slam (winning each major tournament at least once). In 2012, Federer reclaimed the world number one ranking at age 30. In interviews, he has attributed his success and longevity in the sport to an early career decision not to overplay or overextend himself by accepting every invitation, whether for tournament play or sponsorship opportunities. He takes necessary time away from the sport to stay mentally and physically fresh, meaning he continues to enjoy what he does.

Chip Beck is a professional golfer who has enjoyed a long career in his sport at the highest level. He is 56 years old and still competing well on the Champions Tour. During his career, Beck has been a three-time all-American at the University of Georgia, has four victories on the PGA Tour, has won the Vardon Trophy for the lowest scoring average, and was a three-time Ryder Cup participant. Furthermore, he fired a 59 in the third round of the 1991 Las Vegas Invitational, and is currently one of only six players in the history of the PGA Tour to post this record-low number for 18 holes.

Recently, Beck was kind enough to share his thoughts on longterm career success. He noted that golf is unique among professional sports because of the potential longevity of a career, and provided the following comparison: "Michael Jordan played in the NBA for thirteen years, which is nothing compared to many golfers that compete for thirty years at a very high level." Five-time British Open Champion Tom Watson is a case in point. At almost 60 years of age, Watson just missed winning the British Open of 2009 on the 72nd hole, eventually losing a four-hole playoff to Stuart Cink.

During our conversation, I was struck by Beck's competitive passion, which still burns brightly after a lifetime in golf. He touched on several key areas of performance, such as the psychological, physical, and technical aspects, all necessary for achieving long-term success:

> The mental side is the biggest factor. Having a phobic response with the driver will knock you out of golf quicker than anything else, such as when stepping up on the tee and thinking, "This is really difficult," or that you're going to miss the shot. It is important to have one thought that ties your swing together from start to finish without any interruption in thought. That's why tempo thoughts and visual images really work. Great players like Jack Nicklaus and Hale Irwin also stuck with one teacher. They never tried more than one thing at a time and kept their swing mechanics very simple, not making too much change too quickly. Not having the physical gifts of some players, the discipline to get out and exercise regularly and to always stay fit has extended my career. Long term you're better off if you can always stay in shape.

Like most veteran world-class athletes, Beck has endured many highs and lows in his career. He went through an especially rough patch late in his PGA Tour career when, from 1997 to 1998, he missed a near-record 46 consecutive PGA Tour cuts. He acknowledged that he had become burned out from the intensity of tournament play and that he should have taken a 3- to 6-month break prior to that period. Moreover, he added, proper rest is essential for high-level performance. He explained, "You can't push, push, push all the time. You need to be rested and ready. It's like the rest in music is sometimes more important than the music itself."

"Frequent fliers" at the Olympics. A small number of the world's

athletes ever compete in the Olympic Games; an even smaller percentage participate in multiple games. In fact, according to Wikipedia, fewer than 500 athletes have competed in five or more Olympic Games from Athens 1896 to Vancouver 2010. Just over 100 of these athletes have gone on to make a sixth Olympic appearance. Canadian equestrian Ian Millar holds the record with 10 Olympic appearances.

An athlete's longevity and consistency at the top of his or her sport, which is often displayed by those athletes who have made the Olympics and perhaps even participated in multiple games, is by choice, not by chance. These individuals remain motivated to always becoming better athletes. They love learning, training, and competing. They surround themselves with positive people and seek and ask for help. Let's now shine our spotlight on some remarkable athletes who made numerous appearances at the Olympics to learn how they were personally able to maintain their success.

Mark Grimmette is currently the sport program director and head coach for USA Luge. As a luger, Grimmette competed from 1990 to 2010, including participating in five Winter Olympics. He won two medals in the men's doubles event with a bronze in Nagano in 1998 and silver in Salt Lake City in 2002. He carried the United States flag leading the Olympic team into the opening ceremonies at the 2010 Winter Olympics in Vancouver. I asked him how he was able to compete at such a high level for two full decades. He explained:

> First and foremost, luge was my passion; I loved the sport. Secondly, I had a drive to better myself. While my love of the sport influenced how long I was a competitive luge athlete, the combination of my passion and drive to improve myself gave me the motivation to work through adversity and reach success throughout my career. A very important

element to my success, though, was that no matter how experienced at the sport I became, I remained coachable. Those around me contributed greatly to my success.

Peter Westbrook qualified for every U.S. Olympic fencing team from 1976 to 1996. The six-time member of the U.S. Olympic Team won the bronze medal in the men's individual saber event at the 1984 Los Angeles Olympics. Westbrook is also a 13-time U.S. national saber-fencing champion. He shared with me how he was able to maintain his success over the long haul. He explained:

> I was able to receive pay from my job while I was travel-ing to competition. I had such a tremendous love for the sport of fencing that it made it easier to dedicate my whole life to it for so many decades. I had to develop a strong spiritual side of myself in order to go for six Olym-pic Games. If I did not it would have been impossible. Now that love for Olympic competition has been trans-formed to giving it to thousands of kids and seeing their love and dedication transform them into Olympians, Olympic medalists, and great contributors to society.

In addition to financial support, love of fencing, and a strong spiritual side, Peter says he went through the same mental and physical routine before and during every competition. The purpose of his routine was to put his "mind and emotions in the moment, not in the future," while he was competing. He said, "I would imagine myself as a magnificently trained robot ready for optimal performance."

Fight against Father Time. Superstar athletes approach their careers with an emphasis on long-term success rather than quick fix approaches. Here are some impressive examples of mentally and physically fit athletes who stayed on top for a long time:

- Over the course of his 21-year NBA career, Robert Parish was an all-star selection nine times and won three championships with the Boston Celtics and one with the Chicago Bulls.

- Over the course of his 20-year NFL career, Jerry Rice scored a record 208 touchdowns and was rated the best football player of all time by NFL.com.

- Over the course of her 25-year tennis career, Billie Jean King won 129 singles titles and was the number one ranked player in the world on six separate occasions.

- Over the course of his 25-year NHL career, Mark Messier won six Stanley Cups, five with the Edmonton Oilers and one with the New York Rangers.

- Over the course of his 27-year MLB career, Nolan Ryan won 324 games and threw seven no-hitters.

Age is not an impediment to success. For instance, Martin Brodeur, the 41-year-old goalie for the NHL's New Jersey Devils, was still at the top of his game in 2013, his 20th season in the league. Swimmer Dara Torres was a 12-time Olympic medalist. She competed in five different Olympic Games, including the Beijing Olympics in 2008 at age 41. In 2013, light heavyweight boxer Bernard Hopkins broke his own record by becoming the oldest man, at age 48, to win a world title with a unanimous decision over Tavoris Cloud, an opponent 17 years his junior.

Sam Snead won the 1965 Greater Greensboro Open on the PGA Tour at age 52. Leroy "Satchel" Paige, who began his career in the Negro Leagues, was, at the age of 42, the oldest rookie to play in Major League Baseball. He came back to pitch one game in the majors in 1965, at age 59. Satchel famously quipped, "Age is a case of mind over matter. If you don't mind, it don't matter."

The philosophy of mind over matter is exactly what Keiko

Fukuda, a Japanese-born granddaughter of a samurai, must have adopted to become, at the age of 98, the only woman ever to attain the 10th dan, the highest-degree black belt in judo. She is the only woman in the world and the only person in the United States to reach that status. The same can be said for Indian-born British citizen Fauja Singh, nicknamed the "Turban Tornado," who became the first 100-year-old to run a full marathon, completing the 2011 Toronto Waterfront Marathon in 8 hours, 25 minutes.

In terms of the Olympic Games, the oldest modern Olympian is Swedish shooter Oscar Swahn. He won a silver medal at the 1920 Antwerp Olympics at age 72. Swahn is also the oldest participant to win a gold medal, claiming victory at age 64 at the 1908 London Olympics. British archer Sybil Newall is the oldest woman ever to win an Olympic gold medal, achieving this feat during the 1908 London Olympics at age 53.

From soccer's Lionel Messi to golf's Chip Beck, staying power—durability and longevity at the highest levels—takes commitment and attention to detail that goes beyond the physical; it involves sustained obsession, a support system, and resilience in the face of adversity. Examples of adversity include injuries, demotions, and adapting to a new role.

Remember why you play. Do today in training what other athletes won't do. Rest, relax, and restore to avoid burnout. Maintain a constant focus on improvement by looking for ways to progress in every area of your game. Knowing this, ask yourself, "Am I a chicken or a pig; am I just along for the ride, or am I *all-in*?"

EPILOGUE:
THE ULTIMATE VICTORY
IS YOURS

The ultimate is not to win, but to reach within the depths
of your capabilities and to compete against yourself to
the greatest extent possible. When you do that, you have dignity.
You have the pride. You can walk about with character and pride
no matter in what place you happen to finish.

—BILLY MILLS, OLYMPIC GOLD MEDALIST

Our desire to better ourselves and develop our natural gifts is what makes us all distinctly human. We all want to be successful in our most important and competitive pursuits. All of us want to test our talents against others' talents and remain dedicated to our highest achievement. All of us want to perform at our best by competing against our own standard of excellence. Indeed, many of us also want to prove that our best is better than the rest.

No one can play better than their best, but they can certainly play less than their best. Sadly, the latter is too common. Although we all have physical limits, our mind-set is limitless in determining whether we are maximizing our capabilities and potential and whether our limits have been reached. Therefore, the primary goal for athletes is to get and stay in a champion's mind-set each and every time they step on the practice or game field. All athletes can and should strive for personal best performances to see whether they can extend their own awareness of what is possible.

The Latin proverb *Audentes fortuna iuvat* means "Fortune favors the bold." Following the champion principles outlined in this book will ensure that you have that same boldness for your athletic challenges: You will be ready to become everything you're supposed to be because excellence favors the champions. Fire away with the mental and emotional arsenal that you've stockpiled.

Never one to rest on his or her laurels, the champion constantly strives to achieve greater mastery and break personal barriers. Bring with you to practice and games an undying passion and commitment for competitive greatness. Think, "My personal best was good enough only for yesterday." Or, "I can only achieve my personal best today—yesterday's gone."

"A champion needs a motivation above and beyond winning," said Pat Riley, one of the greatest coaches in the history of basketball. He or she seeks greater mastery not so much for external results, such as a monetary reward or societal approval, but rather for an inner sense of personal achievement and satisfaction. He or she competes mainly for the love of the sport and to discover what is possible.

The aim of the champion is to express and elevate one's self by being brilliant at doing what is enjoyed and valued most. Al Oerter won gold medals in the discus throw at four consecutive Olympics from 1956 to 1968. He explained, "I didn't set out to beat the world; I just set out to do my absolute best." We all become better and increase our chances of success by fully being ourselves. Happiness in whatever you do can be achieved only as a by-product of continuous involvement and improvement in the endeavors we deem important.

Do you view a loss through the dual lens of *loser* and *learner*? The perfect performance or event is the one in which, when the whistle blows or you cross the finish line or the workout ends, you can honestly say that you gave your absolute best, regardless of the outcome or externally measured result. Each time, you will either win or learn something new that will make you stronger for the next effort. Just remember to chalk up disappointments to the learning and development process, and then shift your focus to preparing for the next competition.

Record-setting short-track speed skater Apolo Ohno is an eight-time Olympic medalist (including two gold medals). His philosophy is making the most of his life and achieving his absolute best. In his book *Zero Regrets: Be Greater Than Yesterday*, Ohno offered his own definition of winning:

> Winning does not always mean coming in first. Second or third, even fourth—they are wins, too, no matter what anyone says. Real victory is in arriving at the finish line with no regrets. You go all out. And then you accept the consequences.

Nothing beats the inner peace of mind of knowing that you went all out with your best attitude and expended your full effort. Never let yourself lose because you gave less than your best attitude or effort during a game. Remember, only you can control your attitude and effort. So, always compete against your absolute best—regardless of what's on the scoreboard or where your team happens to be in the standings. Doing your best by discovering the borders of your physical limits is also your own true gauge of personal success.

A valuable life—and sports psychology—lesson comes from the teachings of the Buddha:

> It is better to conquer yourself than to win a thousand
> battles. Then the victory is yours. It cannot be taken
> from you, not by angels or by demons, heaven or hell.

For an athlete, conquering yourself means developing a champion's mind-set. Do not allow self-doubt and negative thoughts to hold you back from playing how you really want to play.

To move forward, catch yourself when you are mentally unfocused or physically coasting and reaffirm your commitment to being a champion by striving to compete at your best level. Utilize any momentary negative emotions, such as anxiety or boredom, as important cues to immediately resurrect your champion's mind-set and put your attitude and effort into high gear. Reaffirm that you are in control and still running the show.

Whatever you are faced with is an opportunity to excel. So rise up to meet the challenge of the moment, whatever it is. Compete to your fullest effort and ability, then reap the benefits of this more resourceful way of responding to life's events. The more you practice making this shift and succeed, the more permanent your champion's mind-set becomes.

The champion's journey—the quest toward your best or gold self—is entirely worthwhile yet undeniably hard. You must hold yourself to higher standards both on and off the field. You have to make going above and beyond the rule, not the exception. You need to focus your energy on achieving daily acts of excellence. You must maintain a stick-to-what's-in-front-of-me mentality during competition despite distractions or doubts.

Have the boldness to pursue what you want most in both sports and life. If you have the courage to start, you will have the courage to finish. Make "Think gold and never settle for silver" your life's mantra and put it into daily action. Fully unfurl the potential of your life—both on and off the field—because your life is unique.

Thinking this way is the ultimate victory for *any* champion. Now you are ready to take the champion's honor pledge:

> By my efforts, I will keep my body *strong,* my mind *focused,* and my determination *unstoppable.*
>
> I resolve to compete in the present with power, purpose, and passion.
>
> I know that every sore muscle and drop of sweat is an investment in excellence.
>
> I strive to be my best, nothing less, and joy will come from my striving.
>
> True, pain always comes, but I can endure it.
>
> My body wins when my mind refuses to give in.
>
> In defeat, I will reflect and learn.
>
> In victory, I will savor the glorious moment.
>
> Tomorrow, my *efforts* always begin anew.

APPENDIX A

BE A CHAMPION STUDENT-ATHLETE

Teachers open the door. You enter by yourself.
—CHINESE PROVERB

1. Show up to *every* class and be on time, whether you feel like doing it or not.

2. Pay close attention during class by taking good notes.

3. Pipe up—ask questions during class, form study groups, and meet with your teachers as needed.

4. Study a little bit *each day* rather than cramming at the end. Train your brain to be ready to work at certain, consistent times.

5. Earn good grades by working hard and smart—there are no shortcuts or magic tricks for success. Don't cut corners on your education.

6. Believe that you can excel in any subject if you put your mind to it.

7. Make school a sport and compete in the classroom by viewing your assignments as a challenge to meet. Competition along with cooperation makes everyone better.

APPENDIX B

BE A CHAMPION SLEEPER

1. What amount of sleep helps you feel good? The key is to get the amount of sleep that *you* need. Research suggests a minimum of 8 hours for most people.

2. Give yourself some downtime to unwind before bed. Just before bedtime is not the time to solve problems. Avoid watching television or surfing the Internet during the hour before bedtime. If you are keyed up, find the most boring book or article you can and read a few pages to get sleepy.

3. Turn off or dim any overhead lights as you near bedtime. Otherwise, your brain will still think it is daytime. Use a sleep mask and earplugs if needed to tune out noise and light.

4. Think about what you want to dream about, rather than dwelling on what happened earlier today or worrying about what is on tomorrow's agenda.

5. Choose an idea or key word that will be helpful or calming, and then repeat it over and over again until you fall asleep.

6. Use the 15-second breathing technique and other stress reduction strategies outlined in the book.

7. If you are having a lot of difficulty falling asleep, don't waste your precious time in bed. Get out of bed and do the most enjoyable things you can think of until you are exhausted.

REFERENCES AND
RECOMMENDED READING

Asch, Solomon E. "Effects of Group Pressure upon the Modification and Distortion of Judgements." In *Groups, Leadership and Men,* edited by Harold Guetzkow, 177–90. Pittsburgh: Carnegie Press, 1951.

Bandura, Albert, ed., *Social Learning Theory.* Englewood Cliffs, NJ: Prentice Hall, 1977.

Brooks, Amber, and Leon Lack. "A Brief Afternoon Nap Following Nocturnal Sleep Restriction: Which Nap Duration Is Most Recuperative?" *Sleep* 29, no. 6 (2006): 831–40.

Carney, Dana R., Amy J. C. Cuddy, and Andy J. Yap. "Power Posing: Brief Nonverbal Displays Affect Neuroendocrine Levels and Risk Tolerance." *Psychological Science* 21, no. 10 (October 2010): 1363–68.

Clabby, John. "Helping Depressed Adolescents: A Menu of Cognitive-Behavioral Techniques for Primary Care." *Primary Care Companion to the Journal of Clinical Psychiatry* 8, no. 3 (2006): 131–41.

Craig, Jim, and Yaeger, Don. *Gold Medal Strategies: Business Lessons from America's Miracle Team.* Hoboken, NJ: Wiley, 2011.

Davis, Henry IV, Mario Liotti, Elton T. Ngan, Todd S. Woodward, Jared X. Van Snellenberg, Sari M. van Anders, Aynsley Smith, and Helen S. Mayberg. "fMRI BOLD Signal Changes in Elite Swimmers While Viewing Videos of Personal Failure." *Brain Imaging and Behavior* 2 (2008): 84–93.

Dweck, Carol S. *Mindset: The New Psychology of Success.* New York: Random House, 2006.

Emmons, Robert A., and Michael E. McCullough. "Counting Blessings versus Burdens: An Experimental Investigation of Gratitude and Subjective Well-Being in Daily Life." *Journal of Personality and Social Psychology* 84, no. 2 (2003): 377–89.

Feltz, Deborah L., and Daniel M. Landers. "The Effects of Mental Practice on Motor Skill Learning: A Meta-Analysis." *Journal of Sport & Exercise Psychology* 5, no. 1 (1983): 25–57.

Green, Shawn, with Gordon McAlpine. *The Way of Baseball: Finding Stillness at 95 mph.* New York: Simon & Schuster, 2011.

Hatzigeorgiadis, Antonis, Nikos Zourbanos, Evangelos Galanis, and Yiannis Theodorakis. "Self-Talk and Sports Performance: A Meta-Analysis." *Perspectives on Psychological Science* 6, no 4 (July 2011): 348–56.

Herrigel, Eugen. *Zen in the Art of Archery.* New York: Pantheon Books, 1953.

Holmes, Kelly. *Just Go For It! 6 Simple Steps to Achieve Success.* London: Hay House, 2011.

Hölzel, Britta, James Carmody, Mark Vangel, Christina Congleton, Sita M. Yerramsetti, Tim Gard, and Sara W. Lazar. "Mindfulness Practice Leads to Increases in Regional Brain Gray Matter Density." *Psychiatry Research: Neuroimaging* 191 (2011): 36–43.

Kabat-Zinn, Jon. *Wherever You Go, There You Are: Mindfulness Meditation in Everyday Life.* New York: Hyperion, 2005.

Knight, Camilla J., Candice M. Boden, and Nicholas L. Holt. "Junior Tennis Players' Preferences for Parental Behaviors." *Journal of Applied Sport Psychology* 22, no. 4 (2010): 377–91.

Lewis, Brad Alan. *Wanted: Rowing Coach.* Shark Press, 2007.

Luders, Eileen, Arthur W. Toga, Natasha Lepore, and Christian Gaser, "The Underlying Anatomical Correlates of Long-Term Meditation: Larger Hippocampal and Frontal Volumes of Gray Matter." *NeuroImage* 45, no. 3 (April 15, 2009): 672–78.

May-Treanor, Misty, and Jill Lieber Steeg. *Misty: My Journey Through Volleyball and Life.* New York: Scribner, 2011.

Mischel, Walter, Yuichi Shoda, and Monica L. Rodriguez. "Delay of Gratification in Children." *Science 244*, no. 4907 (May 26, 1989): 933–38.

Murakami, Haruki. *What I Talk About When I Talk About Running: A Memoir.* New York: Vintage, 2009.

Ohno, Apolo. *Zero Regrets: Be Greater Than Yesterday.* New York: Atria, 2010.

Pedroia, Dustin, with Edward J. Delaney. *Born to Play: My Life in the Game.* New York: Gallery, 2010.

Phelps, Michael, with Alan Abrahamson. *No Limits: The Will to Succeed.* New York: Free Press, 2009.

Rotella, Bob, with Bob Cullen. *Golf Is Not a Game of Perfect.* New York: Simon & Schuster, 1995.

Stewart, Mark. *Kobe Bryant: Hard to the Hoop.* Millbrook Press, 2000.

Strack, Fritz, Leonard L. Martin, and Sabine Stepper. "Inhibiting and Facilitating Conditions of the Human Smile: A Nonobtrusive Test of the Facial Feedback Hypothesis." *Journal of Personality and Social Psychology* 54, no. 5 (May 1989): 768–77.

Tang, Yi-Yuan, Qilin Lu, Ming Fan, Yihong Yang, and Michael I. Posner. "Mechanisms of White Matter Changes Induced by Meditation." *Proceedings of the National Academy of Sciences of the United States of America* 109, no. 26 (2012): 10570–74.

Triplett, Norman. "The Dynamogenic Factors in Pacemaking and Competition." *American Journal of Psychology* 9, no. 4 (July 1898): 507–33.

Verstegen, Mark, and Pete Williams. *Core Performance: The Revolutionary Workout Program to Transform Your Body and Your Life*. New York: Rodale, 2005.

———. *Core Performance Endurance: A New Fitness and Nutrition Program That Revolutionizes Your Workouts*. New York: Rodale, 2008.

———. *Core Performance Essentials: The Revolutionary Nutrition and Exercise Plan Adapted for Everyday Use*. New York: Rodale, 2006.

———. *Core Performance Golf: The Revolutionary Training and Nutrition Program for Success On and Off the Course*. New York: Rodale, 2008.

———. *Core Performance Women: Burn Fat and Build Lean Muscle*. New York: Rodale, 2009.

Wooden, John, and Steve Jamison. *Wooden on Leadership: How to Create a Winning Organization*. New York: McGraw-Hill, 2005.

ACKNOWLEDGMENTS

I would like to thank my world-class agent, Helen Zimmermann, for her confidence in this project and all she did to help turn my dream of writing this book into a reality.

I am grateful to Ursula Cary, my editor, for her vision and solid editorial guidance. I'd also like to thank Erin Williams, Chris Rhoads, Jess Fromm, Brent Gallenberger, Emily Weber, and the rest of the winning team at Rodale Books.

Special thanks to the Olympic champions who shared their personal and inspirational stories: Duncan Armstrong, John Montgomery, Gabriele Cipollone, Adam Kreek, Dana Hee, Nick Hysong, Phil Mahre, Natalie Cook, and Glenroy Gilbert.

Thanks also go to Jim Craig, Dr. Gary Hall, Sr., Duff Gibson, Steve Backley, Curt Tomasevicz, Sheila Taormina, Dr. Jose Antonio, Amanda Sage, Brad Alan Lewis, Bob Tewksbury, Chip Beck, Mark Grimmette, and Peter Westbrook for their excellent contributions.

I am especially indebted to the many elite athletes and coaches through the years who have taught me so much about developing a champion's mind and winning the game from within.

Above all, to my wonderful family: my wife, Anne, and our daughter, Maria Paz. They make my life so very special.

INDEX

Underscored page references indicate charts.

A

Aaron, Hank, 211
Abdul-Jabbar, Kareem, 5
Acceptance of self,
    unconditional, 105–6
Acting like a champion,
    12–13
Action, focusing on, 85
Adapting, 25–27, 83–84,
    172–73
Addison, Joseph, 100
Adjustments, making positive,
    25–27
Admiring versus idolizing
    favorite players, 98–99
Adversity, strength from,
    99–100
Affirmation, personal, 62–63.
    See also Self-talk
Aging, 236–38

Ali, Muhammad, 10, 62
Allen, Woody, 118
Allport, Floyd, 145
Anger, channeling, 78
Antonio, Jose, 122
Anxiety, 78, 170
Anxiety management, 51–53
Appreciation, 149–50,
    231–33
Aristotle, 117
Arizona Diamondbacks, 68
Armstrong, Duncan, 180,
    182–85
Asch, Solomon, 142–43
Athlete mode, staying in,
    76–77
Athletes, 1–2. *See also* Champion;
    specific name
Athletic types, 91–93
Attention, 20. *See also* Focus;
    Selective attention

Q

T

U

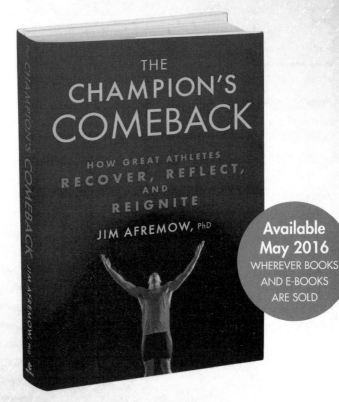